Rosalía
de Castro

New Leaves

ROSALÍA DE CASTRO

New Leaves

Translated from Galician by **Erín Moure**

XUNTA DE GALICIA   Small Stations Press

Small Stations Press
Registered address: 20 Dimitar Manov Street, 1408 Sofia, Bulgaria
You can order books and contact the publisher at
www.smallstations.com

Translator's introduction and English translation © Erín Moure, 2016
Design © Yana Levieva, 2016
© Small Stations Press, 2016
© Xunta de Galicia, 2016

First published in Galician as *Follas novas* by La Propaganda Literaria, Havana, in 1880. This translation follows the 1880 edition, the only one in the author's lifetime.

The publishers gratefully acknowledge the use of the cover image of Rosalía de Castro by Joseph Sellier Loup supplied by the archive of the Royal Galician Academy (www.academia.gal).

ISBN 978-954-384-058-8
Legal deposit C 1066-2016
All rights reserved. The content of this work is protected by the law, which prohibits the reproduction, plagiarism, distribution or public communication, in whole or in part, of a literary, artistic or scientific work, or its transformation, interpretation or artistic performance fixed in any kind of medium or communicated through any means, without the proper authorization.

Contents

Translator's Introduction: We Can Only Read as
Contemporaries: Rosalía de Castro in English 11

NEW LEAVES

Dedication 27
Prologue to the 1880 Edition by Emilio Castelar 29
A Few Words from the Author 43

I
VAGARIES

I. Of women who write of doves and flowers 51
II. I know well there's naught 52
III. Just like clouds 53
IV. You'll say of these lines, and it's true 54
V. *New Leaves!!* It makes me laugh 55
VI. What's this buzz around me?? 56
VII. Some say: my land! 57
VIII. At night's apèx, there 58
IX. Peace, peace so craved 59
X. I once had a nail 60
XI. When one's very joyful, very joyful 61
XII. Today or tomorrow, who knows when? 62
XIII. With no rancour or disdain 63
XIV. That hum of song and laughter 64
XV. For each beat, another 66
XVI. When it was winter 67
XVII. But see that my heart 68
XVIII. With its deaföning and constant mormur 69
XIX. I go in search of honey and freshness 70
XX. Silence! 71

II
INTIMACIES

Farewell! 75
Field crickets, mole crickets, pale wee cicadas 76
How the clouds in open space 77
Rich or poor, back then 78
In the Cathredal 79
Race on, serene and crystal waves 82
Every night I pondered tearful 83
Yesterday You, Tomorrow Me 84
May this cup from which you drink 85
Good Loves 86
Mean Loves 87
Open wide, new roses 88
No Charge 89
Who Wouldn't Sigh 90
They howled at me as I walked on 91
Why, sweet soul of mine 93
The Peal of Dawn 94
Sea! with your fathomless waters 96
Dig quickly, dig down 97
When I think you've gone 98
Luck Betrays 99
Lead me to that clear fountain 100
At the Manor of A… 101
In the skies, blue so clear 102
The Hand of Justice 103
God's cast a veil over 105
Tick-tock, tick-tock! In night's silence 106
Old Friends 107
In the sway of May, long May 109
Faded Moon 110
How placidly they glow 111
Stranger in Her Own Land 112
Padrón…! Padrón…! 114

Keep Going   117
Why, God of pity   118
She's Alone!   119

III
VARIETIES

Of Any Curse, There's No Worse (Than Heartbreak)   123
Time to Get Drinking   130
A true love is greát and blessed   131
Don't sing, don't cry, don't laugh, don't talk   132
Alert!   133
Not in the Dark!   134
Immense elms, myrtles   136
To Everything Its Time   138
Beside the flowers, the girl   139
A Rolling Stone   142
Woe   143
And so! When your most   146
Unnestled   147
I Crave You, You Crave Another   148
Be brave! For though you're pliable as wax   151
Sweet Sleep   152
Scared, I see the abyss   153
For life and for death   154
At the Tomb of English General Sir John Moore   155
With what grace you sway   160
Without Earth   163
Some see black   164
Sad Recollections   166
Frigíd months of winter   170
It was in the month of May   171
What's Up?   176
You, charming and white as snow   177
Ruins (*translation of Ventura Ruiz de Aguilera*)   178

Squeal of carts from Ponte 181
Mandolin Song 182
Pallid virgins with candid faces 184
Vanity 185
Hurry, Álvaro of Anido 186
You claim that marriage 187
Now hair of black 188
May you end up, by God 189
I've a sickness that's incurable 190
Pleasure, for scabies, relieves the itch 191
It's true any person can 192
You write some verses and… what verses! 193
A child trembles in the damp portal 194

IV

HOMELAND

Hush! 199
My sweet abode, my hearth 200
Prideful 203
Poor woman so deaf…! 205
Shane 215
The Magic Flagstone 217
We loathed each other so much 225
In Cornes 229
San Lourenzo Convent 232

V

WIDOWS OF THE LIVING, WIDOWS OF THE DEAD

On to Havana! 237
Never Mind the Dead! 241
Our Home and Native Land! 244
I wove my cloth alone 250

Springs do run dry   251
His Pain's No Pain of Mine   252
Just as meat's sold in the market   253
It was a bone dry Easter, then   254
I will not tend the roses   255
I bear an ache   256
My thoughts, how crazily you fly!   258
I've Lived to See It   259
Not Death's Wake   261
I want to leave, to leave   263
My purest perfume   264
Doctor, her head aches   265
Though you serve me Ribeiro wine of Avia   266
From here I see the pathway   267
In the Cloisters   269
How her heárt aches   271
The sun come to warm me   272
Always you await death   273
What'll I Tell Her?   274
I have a nestful of crazy thoughts   276
One Death Will Do   278
Torres de Oeste   279
Why?   283
She's dying of yearning   284
Oh, Rosa, take heart   285
Burden of Sorrow   288
So Alone   290

Translator's Acknowledgements   292

Index of Titles/First Lines   293

Index of Titles/First Lines in Galician   296

We Can Only Read as Contemporaries: Rosalía de Castro in English

> *Poetry abhors the lie. The lies we are told, they pile up, they become truth by virtue of the heap. By their volume. By virtue of constant recapitulation ... Poetry digs through. Its castings make some growth possible on contaminated ground.*
>
> C.D. Wright

> *Scholars of political emotion and publics need better tools to think about multiple registers of the social/political, rather than presuming that dramatic intensities and orchestrated events are of greater significance than diffused, unaccounted-for, loosely organized, comic, or episodic forms of life.*
>
> Lauren Berlant

One question resonates amid the leaves: *why should we read Rosalía de Castro in English today?* I only translate a book of poetry if the resonant question has a useful echo. Translating poetry as anthropology, as a way of reconstructing a remote place or nation doesn't really interest me. I like my poetry alive in the mouth, and I believe that any time we open a book, we must read as contemporaries. Rosalía de Castro is no exception: when we open the book to read her in English, she has to address us today.

New Leaves exists, so the resonant question does have a useful echo. For one, poetry is perhaps one of those 'better tools' which the renowned philosopher of affect, Lauren Berlant, says we need; it is one of those tools that allows us to think. It is a concentrated movement in rhythm and idiom that propels thinking far more effectively than do the movements of logics and counterlogics. Poetry is the taste of thinking in the mouth. And, as the late American poet C.D. Wright pointed out, poetry makes some growth possible despite the contaminated ground on which we stand and the lies we are forced to consume.

Here I interleave Jacques Rancière, French philosopher of aesthetics and the social, with Berlant and Wright; Rancière defines art as a 'mutation in the fabric of the sensible.' (*Aisthesis*, 11) The art of Rosalía de Castro was, in her century, one of those mutations of the sensible, and one that continues to resonate powerfully in Galicia today. And as Rancière indicates: 'These transformations oblige the modification of the paradigms of art.'[1] (11)

New Leaves was first published in 1880, not in Galicia but in Havana, Cuba, in the colonized new world. Though emigrants maintained strong ties to Galicia and to Galician particularity, their world was also one in which their migration, forced mainly by economics, broke apart the land they left behind. This breaking is inscribed in Rosalía de Castro's work. In her poems, we read the effects of precarity and migration, particularly on women and children. As such, de Castro addresses us today.

Rosalía de Castro in Galician Culture

De Castro and her poetry are iconic in Galicia, and the construction of 'Rosalía' as a totemic figure throughout the late nineteenth and most of the twentieth century is inseparable from the construction of the Galician nation. Both were depicted as melancholic, as cloudy and drizzly as the climate that makes Galicia green. Literary scholar Helena Miguélez-Carballeira is one critical thinker who has written extensively, above all in her *Galicia, a Sentimental Nation:*

---

[1] '... telle émergence artistique oblige à modifier les paradigmes de l'art.' My translation.

Gender, Culture and Politics, on the gradual construction of Galicia as sentimental, vulnerable and childish, and thus as feminine, and considers how this construct (which makes it impossible for the centralist state to interact with Galicia as flourishing and determined) is projected, introjected and perfected through the construct of the figure of Rosalía (known by her first name in Galicia) as sentimental and modest, and, in corollary fashion, of the Galician language as ideal for expressing sentiment, not for thinking. The radical materiality of de Castro's writing, her feminism and anti-clericalism (not unrelated), were utterly washed over with these constructs, an effect particularly played up under Francoism and in its aftermath (1936-1975 and beyond).

Miguélez-Carballeira deconstructs the melancholic and modest view of Rosalía de Castro, and offers a lucid analysis of the effects of that discourse on Galician identity and on perception of Galicia by the central state. Other Galician critics have been at work too. In 2012, poet-critic María do Cebreiro Rábade Villar and critic Helena González Fernández published a collection of essays in Barcelona that cast a new look at de Castro's narrative works in the Spanish language. In 2016, the superb new edition in Galician of *New Leaves*, edited and introduced by poet and scholar Anxo Angueira, reflects the new criticism and promulgates a view of Rosalía de Castro as rebellious and contemporary, recognizing the multiplicity of her forms, and her many ways of subverting dominant stereotypes regarding women, thinking, poetry, migration, poverty, language. Both Miguélez-Carballeira's and Angueira's thinking can be usefully read alongside other essays such as those by María do Cebreiro on the constructs of thinking, irony, shade/shadow, and the infinite in de Castro's work. Novelist and translator María Reimóndez has written on the process of institutionalization of a nostalgic definition of the concept of *morriña*—a longing, also called *saudade,* often attributed to Rosalía, though in *New Leaves* she never mentions either word—as an effect and motor of colonization within Spain itself.[2] Outside Galician culture, Sianne Ngai's *Ugly Feelings,* a signal work on the aesthetics of negative emotions in literary modernist works and the effects on agency, is a major useful referent. All these essays, among others, are vital to thinking Rosalía de Castro in the twenty-first century.

Translating Rosalía de Castro: Resistance and Solidarity

I began translating Rosalía de Castro's *New Leaves* at a moment when the solidarity that had founded the euro in Europe seemed to be shattering over the austerity-strangled economy of a shattered Greece, and then, a year later, over the migrancy created by wars and ecological crises in the mid- and near-East and in Africa. My own psyche, as child and grandchild of migrant Europeans driven to North America by war and poverty, is tied to a vision of Euro/European solidarity as a solution to or, at least, bulwark against fascism and ethnocide. Yet, particularly since the Greek crisis, that solidarity has been breaking, leaving a European exoskeleton exposed. At such moments, we have to resist the demonization of countries in crisis, and of migrants travelling (hot upon that crisis) to reach the centres of economic strength where

---

[2] There are other visions of morriña closer to what we today read in Rosalía de Castro. 'The homesickness that Galegos call *saudade,* or *morriña,* is nostalgia for the future, a desire and hunger for what we don't yet have, not grief for what's lost.' is the view of Manuel Rivas, acclaimed Galician writer (Nash). Another and related view, from one of my own essays (Moure): 'Lacanians—to detour a bit—say we seek the *objet a,* the object lost long before desiring comes into play. The impossible object (which is not even an object, an *a*). I think that, yes, we *are* formed out of its existence, but it's important to note that the impossible or lost *a* is not embedded in a past or prior moment; it is an impossible object that accompanies us as a future. It is akin to what Galician writer Manuel Rivas calls an ecology, akin to what he defines as a *saudade do futuro,* literally—or most closely rather than literally, and problematically—*a nostalgia for the future,* but not really our English "nostalgia" which is too stuck in the past. *Saudade,* more closely, is hope-memory-longing-projection. Such *saudade* has an object, but an object that already doesn't exist, that has never existed, yet we carry it with us. Maybe it is us. Our irreducible singularity.'

it may be possible to rebuild shattered lives. Like Rosalía de Castro in her time, I see the economic forces at work in ours as complex and wounding, and migration as a result of the concentration of capital in the hands of the few, leaving the social fabric to entropic forces.

Rosalía de Castro's late nineteenth century, in *New Leaves*, was in part the product of a generalized discouragement among those seeking justice, following political setbacks that shored up the Spanish monarchy and weakened moves toward more democratic rule; de Castro could only have experienced dismay at the consequences of these events on her fellow Galicians. At the same time, she lived through her own struggles with her health and that of her children.

De Castro's poetic vision is unrelenting. Though she does not directly articulate a world that operates on the basis of a different economy and values, she lays bare the materiality of the world she did live in. The 'now' of de Castro's *New Leaves* coincides, eerily, with our 'now.' In her work, we hear her anger, her revolt, and her rejection of conditions that create precarity and migration as she chronicles the life of those left behind: men without the work skills or habits to emigrate, women with and without families, children left in poverty, and the woe of emigration for a woman whose attachment is to her own land.

Rosalía de Castro creates from a base of disenfranchisement that kindles rage. She recognizes that precarity (whether brought about by austerity measures or directly by economic shrinking) causes forced migration. Today, with a planet in ecological transition pushing more people to cities and into the unrest that gives rise to government repressions and to flight, and with the privilege and greed of corporations whose business model requires institutionalized poverty to make a profit, de Castro's ire and her insistence on women's thinking ring clear to us. Rosalía de Castro's *New Leaves* can be read across and through (a Deleuzian line of flight that returns) today's migrations and the reactions to which they have given rise, in Europe, across Europe and North Africa/Western Asia, in particular, but also in Australia with its offshore detention camps, and across the border of Mexico and the USA. All are focal points for undeclared global conflict (including that which simmers beneath the Trump campaign, ongoing in the US primaries as I write) and restiveness resulting from the intersection of climate change (drought in Africa causing movement of peoples) and global flows of capital (oil, arms, minerals, others). In Rosalía de Castro's poems, the migrancy of Galicians, historic and contemporary, speaks not just in the old Spanish currency of the real or the peseta, but in the contemporary currency of the euro, the pound sterling, and the dollar.

Economic precarity affects women more harshly than it affects men, as much in developed societies as in developing ones. Women are still tasked with the greater part of childcare, care for elders and for those with disabilities, and their job mobility is curtailed by their extended role as caregivers much more than it is for men. The gender wage gap also means that women, more often than not, must make do with even less than the average income. Precarity in financial terms leaves more women vulnerable to having to stay in unsafe conditions, i.e. exposed to situations at home, at work, and in the streets where gender violence occurs. All of these consequences of migration and precarity are written into the poetry of Rosalía de Castro.

Vagaries, Frivolities, Follies, Caprices, Foibles, Whimsies

> *Le réel doit être fictionné pour être pensé.*
> Jacques Rancière

New Leaves is organized as five books in one. In her brief introduction in Galician that follows the florid prose of the Spanish introduction by Emilio Castelar and precedes the poems, de Castro mocks with skilled *retranca* or sarcasm the prejudices she faces as a woman. She 'admits' that thinking is not really for women; it's the job of men. She claims that though she tried to write poems that dealt lightly with things, as women should, conditions around her were such that she failed. As such, her book is cobbled together hastily from poems that are better forgotten.

Her introduction is a set-up, a pit-trap for eager wolves. 'Vagaries,' the title of the first 'book' of *New Leaves* that follows her introduction, seems to invoke the lightweight thinking proper to women: our 'frivolities,' 'fancies,' 'whimsies.' But the first poem categorically rejects any stereotyped view of what women should write. Rosalía de Castro has no intention of writing frivolities. By addressing the Virgin of Paloma, a saint of Madrid (centre and capital of Spain) in the poem, she stakes out a claim both political (she is a Galician who won't bow to the centre) and feminist (no writing about flowers and birds). In the next poem, she also rejects the claim that all thoughts have already been thought by men, so there is no use in writing. She aims to plunge into the material tick-tock of human thinking, so as to examine how repetition enables us to continue as humans and maintain a stable subjectivity. In so doing, she insists on the movement of a woman's 'I' in the text, on her own thoughts and her own subjectivity. Far from creating frivolities in the first section of her book, de Castro lays a substrate and argument for women's thinking: a reason for women to speak.

One could usefully invoke Freud here, via Julia Kristeva, via Judith Butler: the condition of a woman as 'lightweight' is a 'constitutive wound,' a marking on the body politic that enacts women as already vulnerated, and thus, in a reverse logic, as vulnerable (like children). Light and vulnerable. Incapable of the impetus of thinking. De Castro points out this vulnerability and shows that it is in fact a vulneration, a wound in the body politic that constitutes and allows or forbids self-reflexivity. She climbs out of this wound, stained but not thwarted by it, so as to think.

Her 'Vagaries' *are* thoughts, and this first book of twenty poems, each titled using roman numerals in relentless succession[3], elucidates and sets out de Castro's insistence on thinking, and on self-reflexivity that is thought-full. She is not the melancholy woman of modest femininity who is at her best writing personal lyric (as Castelar claims) but a firebrand, one who—as in the epigraph from Rancière above—'fictionalizes the real so as to think it.' In keeping with do Cebreiro, Miguélez-Carballeira, and Angueira, I see Rosalía de Castro as part of a lineage of Galician women who think in their work, whose poetry is a radical materiality, a tool or mode of thinking the real, and whose poetry engages thought and philosophy actively, through rhythm, narrative, call and response, lyric, epic, folktale.

The Intimate Socius

> *[Les énoncés] dessinent des communautés aléatoires qui contribuent à la formation de collectifs d'énonciation qui remettent en question la distribution des rôles, des territoires et des langages—en bref, de ces sujets politiques qui remettent en cause le partage donné du sensible.*
>
> Jacques Rancière

De Castro's statement of poetics is followed by the book 'Intimacies,' which offers a poetic thinking of inside and outside, and of their mutually constitutive roles (elaborated more thoroughly in our time by philosophers such as Jacques Derrida, Chantal Mouffe, and Judith Butler). For de Castro, the outside world and inner world interpenetrate; the social is also intimate. Subjectivity is always political,

---

[3] The only poems titled with numbers in the 1880 edition (the one published in RdC's lifetime) are in this first book, 'Vagaries.' The author's roman numerals, here in this book that is also an insistence on thinking, both mark and mock linear logic. In the remaining books of *New Leaves*, the poems are unnumbered and mostly untitled, rejecting such linearity. The numbers in the first section, and lack thereof in the rest, are potent parts of the structure of the book.

and is constituted only through the chance and hazardous relations—both joyful and painful—that constellate communities. As Jacques Rancière says in the quote above, such aleatory communities (and I see these in Rosalía de Castro's poems) 'contribute to the formation of collective enunciations that question the distribution of roles, territories and languages—in short, these political subjects arise and demand a transformation in the way the sensible world is partitioned.'[4]

The third book, 'Varieties,' begins with poems in dramatic form, in dialogues, and includes a Byronic ode to a British general who perished at A Coruña, while retreating through Galicia in an attempt to save his own troops from a bloodbath at the hands of Napoleon's troops. This poem is one half of a dialogue addressing the people of Great Britain, to which there is no answer. Other moments of dialogue occur in poems via her response to the sound of a mandolin and to a group of Galician emigrant workers and their recognizable song. The last poem in this book does not depict dialogue but the failure of dialogue that occurs when one class of people—homeless orphans—is expelled from humanity by those with means, who pass by on their way to worship their God. This poem ends on an ambiguous double reading of the word 'hope.'

The fourth book, 'Homeland,' examines the notion of home, of what a home can be and what a society is in which homes thrive or do not thrive. Here again, we see the play of inside and outside, and the ways in which 'homeland' is constituted and subjectivities formed. The difficulties in Galician homes finally make the poet turn to the beauty of the landscape around these homes with hatred (a rare expression in a 'Romantic' poet that goes against the grain of extolling landscape!) and, in the final poem, with regret at the brutal intrusion of capital. This last poem, *New Leaves'*

---
[4] My translation.

only dated poem, concludes with the words 'March 1880,' the same month and year in which Rosalía de Castro wrote the introduction to her book.

In a sense these two Marches, of introduction and of 'Homeland', bookend *New Leaves*. They make of the book that follows, the fifth book, a book apart, a book lying outside the time of the book. It is a book of migrations and migratory effects on women, the widows. Men line up to leave in the first poem of this book, and women are left behind to work, and to return to thinking. Thinking is what fills the absence when love and hope are missing. And thoughts become anguished: in one later poem, a lonely woman wanders near the western gates to the ocean, the furthest west she can go without emigrating; she speaks to the towers there, the *Torres de Oeste*, and examines suicide—in the face of theological injunctions—as a fair possibility rising from radical solitude. And de Castro's *is* a radical solitude, not the misty *saudade* or nostalgic resignation in the face of loss that was often attributed to her. This radical solitude leads to facing mortality directly, facing the breakage of human life wrought by migrations that, in the absence of political change, presents a radical resolution: the death of subjectivity itself.

A Translator's Decisions

In translating poetry, I tend to work by creating what I call 'soundscapes,' rather than entering into the dualistic battle of rhyme vs. sense, or form vs. meaning. I think it's difficult to turn the variegated forms of de Castro's work into similarly syllabated and rhymed works in English. I myself, when I read her poems, read a kind of rhythmic progress and at times the rhyme is an important part of that, at times not. Soundscape, on the other hand, acknowledges the role played by the ears that listen: to focus on soundscape is to try to recreate the experience of the poem on all its levels. Yet all ears are, of course, acculturated, already formed in their own culture (in learning a second language for example, we can't make a sound that we can't hear, and we tend to hear the sounds of other languages as consistent with what we know, at least at first). In creating Rosalía de Castro's work in English, I worked to let my Canadian ear and English create a soundscape rhythmic enough so that when I read it, I feel it captures the music of Rosalía de Castro (and of 'Rosalía' the icon as well), her material sonic texture.

In this book, as well, I wanted to reflect the variety of spellings in the Galician, for the language in the nineteenth century was not normativized; Rosalía de Castro learned it by ear, and as a result, her orthographies are various and shifting. Part of her poems' modernity and shudder are these very sonorities in her spelling and phrasing, her indents and spacings that make her poetry different from any other of her time or of ours. Her localisms, aural spellings, Castilian inflections are critical to the text: what might seem now as 'deviant' spellings also serve as emotional markings; they are not blemishes but marks of legitimate expression.

In response, I at times create small 'misspellings' in the English, and enact certain nonstandard punctuations, just to provide a wee glimpse of difference to readers. I also vary the words for God, as that vocable resounds differently for a reader in our time than in hers. I wanted to make space for a spirituality that admits a wider range of belief, for though she was anti-clerical, de Castro was not pagan. Another word I've altered is 'negro' which I often translate as 'grey' or in other ways than translating it as 'black,' since in the English of my time, using 'black' as a metaphor for negativity occludes a racism we have to recognize and banish.

Here and there in the text, I've added footnotes to help bring Rosalía de Castro into the present for readers in English. My interventions are few, and should not be considered scholarly. After all, I am a poet-translator responding to a poet, and I respond to de Castro out of my own readings in English (and thus cannot present text as a Galician would read it). If Rosalía de Castro lived and wrote today in English, I think she'd be C.D. Wright, Myung Mi Kim, Bronwen Wallace, Claudia Rankine, NourbeSe Philip, Dorothy Livesay, Elizabeth Bishop, Lisa Robertson, Rita Wong, Dionne Brand. With these poets and others in mind, we can read de Castro as our contemporary in English, and—given *New Leaves* first appeared in Cuba—as a poet of the Americas, one who is also migrant, woman, and far too restless for old Europe. In saying this, I lay claim to Rosalía de Castro as our own poet of hybrid displacement, of the toll of migrancy and poverty, of precarity in the face of capital, and poet of the 'mutation of the sensible' that calls into question the partition of the sensible in our world, thus altering and opening other possibilities, other futures, through ART.

Erín Moure
Montréal and Kelowna, 23 May 2016

FURTHER READINGS (*key)

*Angueira, Anxo. 'Estudo Introdutorio' in *Follas Novas* by Rosalía de Castro, ed. Anxo Angueira. Vigo: Xerais, 2016 (7-99).

*_____. 'Fixación, Notas, e Comentarios' in *Follas Novas* by Rosalía de Castro, ed. Anxo Angueira. Vigo: Xerais, 2016 (347-467).

Butler, Judith. *Gender Trouble: Feminism and the Subversion of Identity.* NY and London: Routledge, 1990.

_____. *Bodies That Matter.* NY and London: Routledge, 1993.

_____. *Excitable Speech: A Politics of the Performative.* NY and London: Routledge, 1997.

_____. *Giving An Account of Oneself.* NY: Fordham U Press, 2005.

*Derrida, Jacques. *L'écriture et la différence.* Paris: Seuil, 1967.

*_____. 'Signature, Event, Context' in *Limited Inc.* Trans. by S. Samuel Weber and Jeffrey Mehlman. Evanston, Il: Northwestern U Press, 1988 (17 and others).

_____. 'Remarks on Deconstruction and Pragmatism,' in *Deconstruction and Pragmatism.* ed. Chantal Mouffe. London: Routledge, 1996 (77-88).

do Cebreiro, María. *Fogar impronunciable. Poesía e pantasma.* Vigo: Galaxia, 2011.

González Fernández, Helena and María do Cebreiro Rábade Villar (eds.) *Canon y subversión. La obra narrativa de Rosalía de Castro.* Barcelona: Icaria, 2012.

*Miguélez-Carballeira, Helena. *Galicia, a Sentimental Nation: Gender, Culture and Politics*, Cardiff: U Wales Press, 2013.

_____. 'Rosalía de Castro: Life, Text and Afterlife' in *The Companion to Galician Culture,* ed. Helena Miguélez-Carballeira. London: Tamesis, 2014 (175-191).

Mouffe, Chantal. *The Democratic Paradox.* NY: Verso, 2000 (12, 21).

Moure, Erín. 'Stakes, Poetry, Today,' *My Beloved Wager.* Edmonton: NeWest Press, 2009 (208).

Nash, Elizabeth. 'Manuel Rivas: Spirits of the Sea,' *The Independent (UK),* 31 January 2003. Web. 22 May 2016.

Ngai, Sianne. *Ugly Feelings.* Cambridge, MA: Harvard U Press, 2005.

*Rancière, Jacques. *Le Partage du sensible.* Paris: Éditions La Fabrique, 2000 (64).

*_____. *Aisthesis: Scènes du régime esthétique de l'art.* Paris: Galilée, 2011 (11).

Reimóndez, María. '[Monolingual] Sounds, [No] Translation as Subversion and the Hope for Polyphony' in *The Transnational Story Hub: Between Self And Other,* Ed. by Merlinda Bobis & Belén Martin-Lucas. Barcelona: Centre d'Estudis Australians, U de Barcelona, 2016 (117-139). Web. 21 May 2016.

New Leaves

TO THE BOARD AND MEMBERS OF THE
SOCIEDADE DE BENEFICENCIA DOS NATURALES
DE GALICIA NA HABANA
[GALICIAN CHARITABLE SOCIETY IN HAVANA]

A feeling of gratitude leads me to dedicate this book of mine to you today. It is the day on which the sons and daughters of Galicia brought into existence one of their most glorious achievements (allow me to say so, for I believe it): the day on which, to universal applause and so far from Galicia, the Galician Charitable Society *was founded, by those who wished to turn their eyes and hearts toward their country, and who, in their act of patriotism, commemorated a book that also was the exalted fruit of love for our country.*

I do know that adding the name of the author of Galician Songs *to the names of the Society's founders (something for which I thank them as it unites me to the charitable work closest to my heart) was nothing more than an expression of love for the absent country about which I wrote, if not good verses, then at least fortunate ones. I know this well, but even so, I feel obliged to make a public gesture of my gratitude, so as to also make public the esteem that my countrymen in Havana have shown me.*

Please accept the dedication, then, of this new book of mine; it speaks of our country and is written in our language. Please accept it, not for what it is worth, but for what it signifies.

Rosalía Castro de Murguía
(Honorary member of the Galician Charitable Society in Havana)
Santiago de Compostela, 23 February 1880

PROLOGUE TO THE 1880 EDITION
translated from Spanish[5]

I enjoy nothing more than roaming the regions of Spain to contemplate the monuments that awaken memories of our forefathers. The past comes alive in the places where tragedies unfolded. The souls of the dead return in the conjurations and evocations of memory, as if they seek the origin of ventures glad or grisly that transcend their names in

---

[5] The curious and voluble text of Emilio Castelar (Spanish politician, author and supporter of a Republic in an era when the monarchy had regained its hold and put down liberalism, and friend of de Castro's husband) is often left out of contemporary Galician editions of *New Leaves*. His Spanish introduction, in a Galician book, was intended to block criticism of Rosalía de Castro, given her anti-clerical views, liberal view of social justice, and treatment of Galicia as a nation. It is a curiosity in many ways, but one that casts light on the construction of Galician identity by centralist Spain. Castelar sees in de Castro only melancholy, and in Galicia only drizzly green and the scent of flowers. He talks lamely of the 'provincial injustices' which should be addressed by central Spain but says not what they are. Apart from 'population density and poor soil,' we learn little of Galicia's problems. But the soil is rich in Galicia; it is landholding constraints and caciquism that strangle people and force them to leave! Castelar does not recognize de Castro's vigour or her anger; he values her intimist lyric poems as 'original' while claiming her socially-engaged work falls short of the mark. As Miguélez-Carballeira notes in her *Galicia: A Sentimental Nation?*, the social construct of Galicia involved the sentimentalizing of women, and the use of the gender binary as a force to put Galicia and its inhabitants in a submissive position. As such, the preface of Castelar, though intended as a 'good housekeeping seal of approval' for this writer who wrote in Galician, acts as a wound or cut. The punctum of Castelar's article occurs early: after speaking as a historian to laud his travels around Spain and say that walking in real places tells us more than does reading history, Castelar admits he has never been to Galicia. Then, hardly skipping a beat, he leaps into inventing a Galicia of soft horizons and mists and green leaves and the songs of birds, all of those climatic things that make Galicia prone to melancholy and sentiment, at least, in the constructs of central Spain. I agree with Anxo Angueira who, in his notes to *Follas Novas* (352), says the Spanish prologue is not at odds with the Galicianity of the book, but indicates Rosalía's literary work inhabited a complex institutional and cultural frame.

the world and their eternal rest. We learn more about the fate of Rome by walking the Appian Way, bordered by tombs, than by studying Livy and Tacitus. More Spanish history lies in the mute stones of the Toledo cathedral than in the grandiloquent pages of Mariana and de Mendoza. The fields of Montiel still bear the curse of the fratricidal Trastamaras; the brambled ruins of Poblet still guard the august shades of Aragonese kings; the heights of Almuradiel continue to reveal their glory to the most vulgar eyes just as they do to sunlight; the peak of Monserrat still reflects the eyes of Catalan navigators of the Mediterranean who raptly greeted it in their fabled expeditions to the east of Europe; the grills of Granada hold the poem of holy war and national Reconquest. There is scarcely a corner of the Peninsula where nature is not marked by grand scenes of history.

As a historian, I've contemplated the main sites of historical fact a thousand times, and still have never seen the places where our modern chronicles began and our national life burst into flower, and where the poem of the Reconquest began as the Spanish language muttered its first words in the resounding cry for God and Liberty, as the chapel of Covadonga appeared as the first among our victories. Here the Asturian and Galician kings repelled the Arabs hurled north by the high noon of deserts, then the Normans spewed from the North Sea, doing so in primitive dialects of such sweetness that even in their austere Romanesque churches we still feel the lilt of our national spirit and touch the wood of our cradle. In other words, I still haven't seen Asturias or Galicia![6]

How many times have I imagined myself there and tried to describe what I see in my mind! Above all, strange and

---

[6] When one reads works by people who *had* been in Galicia, such as the memoirs of the Duke of Wellington and General Sir John Moore regarding the Peninsular War campaign in 1808-1814, they do not wax about green and misty scenery as does Castelar, for the poverty they encountered was great, visible, and problematic. In the midst of Castelar's imaginings and emotings, we bear witness not to a description of reality, but to the construction of Galicia as misty, rural, pretty, and of Rosalía de Castro as meek, modest, sickly, melancholy, i.e. *womanly.*

unknown Galicia called me with its innumerable attractions and wet greenery flecked with seafoam, carpeted with endless meadows, hills of shady forest, flowers aglow at its feet, its shining inlets and ports like quiet lakes, bedecked with chestnut and orange groves, its green seas and horizons blanketed by rolling fogs like a sort of southern Spanish Scotland, ideal, like Britain's Scotland, for poetry and song, and love of Nature.[7]

How amazing it will be to view the cathedral on which the vanishing Middle Ages gazed, and to which pilgrims thronged from as far away as Bulgaria and Russia to be pardoned for their sins upon touching lips to its floor! My soul will be ecstatic in the multihued Portico de Gloria amid lilies like nuances of prayer, gilt burnished like purest ether, in the presence of innumerable figures returned like mystic butterflies from the flowers of heaven, and amid statues like messengers who lift to heaven our resolute aspirations willed to the infinite, proceeding eternally from our pure dark planet! Such shadows are cast on those modest chapels, ancient lodgings for pilgrims and holy end to a stormy journey! How the cries of the soldiers of Clavijo, Calatañazor, Las Navas and Tarifa resound in the domes—invoking the apostle who led our armies on his pale apocalyptic steed! In those times of faith, Jerusalem, Rome, Compostela were the three spiritual steps that brought poor humanity to face the three persons of the Blessed Trinity.

Our spirits comforted by these revered memories, we can turn to nature! I already know we can't expect the north to have the tint of our southern lands or the flaming light that haloes the Giralda in Seville and makes the striations of the Parthenon of Athens glow. I already know that our classical paganism, our spatial forms, our sculptural reliefs, the dry

---

[7] The life of the Spanish mind here includes *imagining* Galicia—and this imagination silences Galicia, turning it into a little Scotland, i.e. a conquered territory of a larger realm. The writer has been to neither Galicia, nor Scotland.

torrents that hold oleander crowned with rosy flowers, and the palms that sway in the blazing heat of the *simoom*,[8] are not found in the green fields touched by constant evaporation of the seas and by beneficial rains, veiled by fog. What will be found is quiet countryside as in Theocritus, meadows that renew their green in perpetual spring, forests of fruit trees laden with sweet orbs, hills where bushes flourish, the ancient village belltower visible through oaks and chestnuts, the huts in deep valleys with cows at the stable door, serene clear inlets meandering full of small boats that contrast with the heavy carts on land where, working incessantly, peasants of both sexes are followed by countless progeny who chorus the sonatas and songs whose tunes we know from the European masters, from Beethoven's pastoral symphony in F Major, op. 68, to Bellini's tender *La Sonnambula*, the classical expression of country joy. Galicia has painters, whom I won't name here, as capable of portraying their land to us as the Málagan painters have done with a lunch in Caleta or the Sevillan painters with a dance in Triana.

In Galician paintings there is no jet-black shadow on chalk-white alabaster walls: light's Galician caress sifts through airy vapours, muffled by exuberant vegetation, without hyperbole, devoid of jarring reverberations, so our eyes receive and enjoy it in ineffable peace. Under the branches of centenary trees across a plaza, surrounded by flowery perfumed honeysuckle and on grasses soft and plush, a Galician mountaineer in cap, breeches and dark felt jacket buttoned and adorned with silver, dances with a beautiful Galician lass, whose bright kerchief billows over an exquisite shawl and dark serge petticoat, necklaces splendid over her white blouse. To the sound of the *gaita*, they weave a sad, loving, voluptuous dance.

Though not hot, this land inspires its children to a passion

---

[8] What he describes as 'ours' is the south of Spain, almost as if that were the 'true Spain.' Galicia and Galician are then thrust outside the 'our.' Castelar imagines Galicia from outside and keeps it outside.

so inflamed it radiates devotion. Neither Catalans proud of being citizens of perfect nationality, nor Andalusians in the most privileged and poetic region of Spain, nor Valencians in their Asiatic gardens, nor the vigorous Aragonese, love their country as do Galicians. The shade of trees, lilt of waters, crust of corn-rye bread, the scent of cows, spaciousness of their counties, bells that toll the angelus as night falls, the melody of their hurdy-gurdies, singers that voice *alboradas*, inhabit their senses, feelings, consciousness, entire soul and being so strongly that if leave they must, they are as uprooted as trees, and slump, stop wishing; their gaze darkens and energy withers, their faces pale and they forget speech and the ache of sadness is so acute in their bodies that death is all their unhappiness allows them. There are races like this so strongly tied to their land that splitting the two is like separating body and soul, and means an end to existence. Most examples of the suicide of entire peoples that so astound us, like those of Numancia and Sagunto, can be explained by an attachment to native soil so powerful that, far from it, people cannot breathe or live. There are nomadic races, such as the invaders from the North, who are propelled by an internal urge to be on the move with the horse-drawn carts that carry them from one territory to another. Conceived in one place, born in another, they live in continual journey, dying without knowing the village where they were born, changing beliefs as they change country; their vocation is emigration and conquest, and with their terrible power they succeed in altering human societies just as air is altered and fields changed by storms or floods. Then there are races who never leave where they were born and who are attached to their place as flesh is to bone. These races suffer homesickness, called nostalgia in Greek, a horrible ailment that almost always ends in death. It seems that destiny wishes it so. Galicians are constantly obliged to emigrate, because of population density and poor soil. Imagine their grief when the horizon is crossed and the belltower of the parish church recedes and vanishes, along with the cemetery where their elders rest, bones mixed with roots of life, and the hearths that sheltered their affections and the passions that kindled their blood and pressed the flesh of the heart. From where the emigrant is headed, he will not return to the lass who, with one hand to her ear, her head swaying, eyes wide from seeking and not finding the beloved, intones the sad Galician lament that corresponds to the Andalusian *zagaleja*, a serenade similar in its long sad cadence to a lullaby of love or sigh of death. It's no surprise that in abandoning places indissolubly tied to their passion, emigrants falter and die. Soul-worn sadness is reflected in their poetry, and it is truly a melancholy poetry of the heart.

Thus Northern poetry has both ambiguity and depth. Nature is reflected in the consciousness of its bards just as objects are in the poems of Ossian. The star that shines in the first shadows of evening, the mist that rises from sea waves to become cloud, hurricane winds that smash on rocky cliffs covered in pine forests, hill grasses that undulate and bend in the kiss of zephyr winds; the torrent that foams between crags, the moon crowned with fog that turns its face pale and mysterious, the caves full of nocturnal birds whose cries mix with the evening call to prayers, all these give Galician poetry the flavour of the canticles of peoples obliged by latitude and climate to shelter inside and relate the phenomena of the outside world to the affections and ideas of the soul.

The Galician language, in the wealth of its vocal combinations, the softness of its consonants, the copious rhymes and variety of metres, the onomatopoeia of its words, is related to all southern languages. Upon hearing it, you'd say you hear Italian, Provençal, Limousin, or any of the languages spoken on the Mediterranean and enriched by the trade between peoples, a language that, to a Helleno-Latin base, adds layers and enhancements, enamels and embossings brought by the natural movement of peoples. Added to these qualities is candour, simplicity, and an archaic flavour of the Middle Ages. Later, in the century that generated great states, when Spain was formed, the Galician language ceded its laurels to the great language of the centre, Castilian. Still, Galicia, by its geography less open than Southern Spain to foreign incursions, less Hellenic and less Arab, for neither exercised power on the shores of the Atlantic as they did on the Mediterranean, yet very Roman during the Empire and even after the Germanic or Swabian invasion, has a more determined complexion and longer tradition than does Spain. Its speech is Latin turned Romance by the Swabians, as Castilian is Latin turned Romance by the inhabitants of the central plain. Make of this what you will; Galicia has a beautiful literature. The most important writer and scholar of the Middle Ages, King Alfonso X, chose Galician for his poetic homage to the Virgin, and the loves and losses of the popular writer Macías are also immortalized in Galician. Examine Galician literature as a whole, and you'll realize that its poets have something of the Swabian school so beloved and lauded in Germany for its fluidity of rhyme, along with its depth of feeling and ideas.

If Galician literature had but one book, *New Leaves* by Rosalía de Castro alone would testify to its glory. Since, like all art, poetry is profoundly felt ideas beautifully expressed, I declare that no one feels more and expresses better. Tenderness entwines with sadness, light with mystery, inspiration with truth, forming a conjunction of such new and original destiny that our understanding never tires of admiring it, though we be tired of the arbitrary conventionality of the schools of artifice that engage in resuscitating dead pasts, or in repeating impure reality like a photograph. Rosalía feels and knows how to express feeling.[9] Her soul does not savour poetry in

---

[9] Above all, this is the job of the 'sweet and primitive tongue,' it seems. And Rosalía de Castro's role is to 'feel,' not to think. This is, of course, a typical view regarding women in her day, especially regarding women who spoke up in public, as if it were an effort to dim their voices. With quiet and forceful Galician sarcasm or *retranca* (deeper and more subtle than English sarcasm), Rosalía reproduces this structure in her introduction as if it were unquestionable, only to blow it apart in the first sequence of poems.

the great, in the immense, in the infinite; like a violet, it loves shade and exhales its aroma with such humility that it finds fault with its own merits. It is rare to see, as in her 'Vagaries', variously-inspired visitations, formless clouds evaporated from heart to mind that at times seem to swirl in the ink of ideas, and at others to blush in the lightning flash of passion. She asks 'why write?' and cannot answer. But in this incapacity is the secret of poetic vocation. Whoever sings regardless, obeying the movement of being as the harp obeys the hand that plucks it, expressing ideas that present themselves instinctively to the mind more through revelation than reflection, this poet receives the gift of poetry from the heavens so as to raise and lay it amid the stones of the earth.

It's no surprise that with this gift comes melancholy. Just as there is no redeemer without crown of thorns, no profit without being consumed in the retort from which new elements emerge, no hero without embracing death, it is impossible to be poet and not suffer with all those who suffer, impossible to not weep with those who weep, to not feel the nostalgia of the mysterious heavens. Rosalía is sad, and sadness is her mystic halo, heard in all the chords of her lyre. Thus the reader weeps when she bids farewell to her meadows, to the cloister where she took rest, to dark mountains silvery in the dawn glow of the Sar and Sarela, to the brown urban towers visible in blurry distances. In bidding them farewell, we realize that they endure, immobile, while those beings who believe themselves superior and immortal compared to objects, as eternal as souls, step each day toward death and leave their illusions and hopes in the tortuous curves of the path. I know of few emotions more masterfully expressed than the awakening in Rosalía's heart on entering the Cathedral of Santiago. We hear old people praying, see the last rays of sun penetrate stained glass and diverge in the brilliant webs of spiders; we feel the terror that grips her when in the plaint of bells we see the suffering souls painted on the altars and the heads of saints moving as if recounting mysteries to one another. Entranced by her evocations, we wonder if the statues' faces have souls, and stony lips words, and if the archbishops and bishops beneath the flagstones have the strength to rise from their cold marble beds and beg pardon from the crucifixes, illuminated by flickering lamps, and if the Lady of Solitude has tears to weep at the sufferings of her divine Son and the eternity of our sins. I can't fully express how much I am moved by the words that Rosalía dedicates to the cemetery, the hermitage, to burial, to religion mixed with death. You'd think her ideas were flowers budding amid tombs. They touch the soul with the languid sadness of willow branches and scent of cypress. The poet does well in singing these abysses where the frenzy of our lives ends and the vertiginous motion of our species comes to a halt. In the valleys of my own land, I've never beheld a church without emotion. A church, sole ideal of the village, where art takes on religious form; mystical nave, populated by saints who intercede for us and are surrounded by the dead who await resurrection; luminous candle, lit upon the ashes of the world, that projects light into the depths of the soul, solitary light that is to us like a mysterious star on a stormy day; ark that floats in the flood of our tears; intersection of the paths of earth and eternity. Influence on every exhalation ascending to the infinite and on all inspiration descending from the infinite, a church always moves us because of the tears evaporated in its air awaiting consolation and because of the cadavers fallen to its floor, awaiting pardon via prayers that flicker under domes and amid votive offerings hung on its walls, via tongues of fire sent by the divine, and clouds of incense offered by the human spirit to the absolute; via the power of arches, stones, altars and cupolas to reveal divine mystery unfolding in the immensity of spaces, that agitates and sets us trembling from the depth of our hearts to the peak of our minds.

I know no composition in any literary language of the Peninsula more tender than Rosalía's *'Padrón...! Padrón...!'*

Soon enough, it will achieve fame as huge as did the immortal composition of Bécquer: 'My God, how lonely the dead are.' Our first thought on contemplating a cemetery is that everything ends in us, as existence passes from youth to maturity and on to death: unending laughter, interminable dances, sweet lullabies, loving colloquia, serene nights, melancholy guitar, the chords of its serenade. In Rosalía's poem, following a sad reflection upon all we carry dead in our own selves, she paints the Adina cemetery as it appeared to her child's eyes, with its dark old olives, its clerics like ancient cypresses that take the sun inside its walls, and the children that flit between tombs like butterflies between flowers. Tombstones stand in the dark monotone of upturned earth; the white charnel house in deepest night emits a phosphoric light from its sumptuous fires; grass, hollyhocks, hemlock and nettles grow green, fed by the dead, exhaling from the surface of the graves the breath of roots mixed with bones, the oxygen of life. Naturally, a small girl's soul feels joy in the cemetery. In this joy lies the profundity of the thinking achieved via the sovereign intuition of the poet. In an age when we no longer see the dead, we don't believe in death. Do we not play at the gates of the cemetery as we do at the gates of school? Has there ever been any more terrible contrast than the games, laughter, and cries of wee orphans while priests intone canticles of eternity at the mourning house door, before the full casket?

In Adina, the girl sees grass over tombs, flowers on grass, butterflies on flowers, sky over birds, and life brims in the temple of death. But the poet, a long time gone, now returns in sadness. When she asks after her beloved dead, no one answers. Time has swirled around them, has depopulated Padrón of its favourites and populated the cemetery with their remains. She runs and looks through the gate, and instead of seeing and hearing what the child sees and hears, she sees upturned earth above which souls wander, and hears bells weep for the dead.

Let us console ourselves. No reality is more repugnant nor ideal so beautiful as death. A corpse, as seen by the body, is filled with worms; to the eyes of the soul, it is encircled by angels. The corpse stinks when we draw near with our bodies, and scents the air with balsam when we approach with our souls. What would become of us if we never died! The doubts that furrow our brow and disappointments that rip the heart, love without hope, the pain of absence: all of it seems eternal. Only on the far side of the tomb will the ideal be true, illusion certainty, poetry thought, thought life, life eternity, eternity unjealous love, fulfillment free of disappointment, beliefs unshadowed, spirits disembodied, art formless, happiness free of worry, being full, justice endure, and the vision of the Eternal be perfect. God, may the empty chalice not reappear; may our beloved never be taken from us; may the abortive birth of gross reality not follow the ideal dreamed with so much love; may we not be frozen by the gale of new heartbreak; no, to the last flowering of illusions and final harvest of hope! If this is to be impossible in the world, kill us quickly in your divine mercy so that soon even our slanderers will act justly and we will sleep forever knowing ourselves blessed and loved, awaiting the flood of tears over our ashes.

One of the most outstanding qualities in Rosalía de Castro is her poetic vision, her intuitive view of the mysterious relation that exists between inner and outer worlds, between the universe composed by humanity and that composed by nature. The sphere that curves the horizon and the sphere of the brain, the light of the eyes and that of the stars, rains and tears, storms and aches, electricity that snakes from the clouds, sympathies we radiate from our being: all form a romance in assonance, an ode in consonance, and a sympathy in tones sharp and flat. The full moon, gazing at Ocean, lifts its tides; the beautiful woman gazing at our eyes lights them afire, which then ignites desire. Magnetic currents, which cause sensitive leaves to fold, have another current that makes nerves vibrate like the strings of a harp. There is, between word and idea, form and background, soul and body, the same relation as between electricity and magnetism, light and heat. The serpent fascinates the wee bird just as meditation fascinates the mystic. In the wilds there are many souls and ecstatic larks. The enthusiasm of hearts contributes to the movement of bodies and to the force of muscles. The inebriated woman would topple in her tracks if she didn't believe that God compels her, and the fortune teller fall dead from her stool if she didn't believe God spoke through her mouth. Human beings cling to others in society just as worlds in outer space hold each other in universal attraction. The gaze of the tiger terrifies us as much as the gaze of our enemy, and the gaze of a sheep awakens our compassion as does the gaze of a child. There is a mysterious relation between nuances of a prism and notes of music. Pythagoras explained more to his disciples through sight than through words. Alexander, who had but 50,000 men in Arbela while Darius had a million, did not want to fight at night as Parmenion advised him, because he trusted more in the prodigies of his eyes than in his tactics. Magnetism, electricity, love, will, heat, passion, light, idea, all these virtues combine, material and spiritual, just as forces combine in the immensity of the universe. Few thinkers and poets better express these relations than Rosalía de Castro in her stunning verses.

To describe her in few words is to say: lyric poet par excellence. When on wings of robust style she creates impersonal, objective poetry, verging on epic, it lacks the originality that distinguishes her when she voices her own emotions and presents the external world in relation to her soul, celestial, luminous, transparent, where the least breeze raises ripples and undulations, the least reflection of light extends brightness that nuances the smallest thing.[10] Trees and humble grass, the hill that remains still and the bird that

---

[10] Here again, Rosalía is allowed but one voice, that of sentiment.

crosses horizons: mirrors flourish and copies and portraits are left us. As lyric poet of excellence, Rosalía is necessarily also elegaic. Throughout her verses, feelings possess her; a melancholic sadness at the universal disappointments of human life, and an exalted sadness at the disappointments particular to Galician life. Man is the synthesis of creation. The universe of outer space gathers its beautiful ether to produce the light in human eyes; electro-mechanical fluids condense their most powerful currents in the cords of our nerves; atoms from the edge of space accumulate in our body to compose the most perfect organism. On top of all these determinations and modes of the material universe, an unutterable, unnarratable, sublime mystery arises in us: that mystery of the soul that slowly begins to see the infinite and to flow out into eternity. Everything thinks of us and suffers in us. Our voice repeats the universal lament of beings who ache from the energy it takes to cross the border and from the fatality that grips us there, as if we were in jail, in prison, in eternal supplication. This lament becomes more acute as we grow and progress, and encounters its poetic echo in all the seasons of *New Leaves*. The grief most beautifully expressed here is the grief and pain of Rosalía's land, Galicia. We realize how its beautiful provinces are kept in isolation by Spain.

We hear the laboured breath of a race forced by bleak social conditions to perform the most physical and painful jobs. Visible are the secular wounds opened in its people by ancient feudal tyranny. Their qualities are notable: sharp intelligence, honed acuity, perpetual sadness. The pain of Galician agonies is repeated in each Rosalian verse: separation, absence, nostalgia, emigration, while the countryside is wet, fresh, green, simple as an idyll, pleasing as a spring morn with its whiffs of fruit and flowers, its rhythms of dulcimer and bagpipe, its clear and peaceful inlets amid arduous hardship and the sorrow of forced exile. All poetic work, subjective and personal as it may seem, is civic work. The aching grief of Galicia speaks through Rosalía, and men of

State, those who have held government in their hands, who handle Government today and may tomorrow hold power, must, touched by voices such as hers, acknowledge that the demands of the provinces are just and require satisfaction, and find remedies to resolve longstanding inveterate ills. We must not forget that not too long ago, a venerable Portuguese writer called the Portuguese, Brazilians and Galicians one literary nation. This might be dismissed as delusionary had so many horrendous crises not occurred, and certain tendencies not been noted which could reappear tomorrow, under absolutism's flag or under the banner of the demagogy that so often wreaks disasters and bitterness. There is no better way to quell exaggerated provincialism than to satisfy provincial demands for justice. We must not forget that regions like Galicia have brilliant literatures of their own, which, in keeping with a law of life, that of variety, can coexist with the national literature, doing no harm to the country, for Spain has increased greatness when its children flourish, when the organs that compose its body are strong, and when the stars in its skies are more brilliant.

With her books of poetry in Galician, Rosalía de Castro is a star of first magnitude in the vast firmament of Spanish art.[11]

Emilio Castelar

---

[11] A permissible role for the rebellious Rosalía is this: to be subsumed into Spanish art, where she can be seen as a side note, a quirk of peninsular culture, rather than seeing her as central to Galician culture.

A FEW WORDS FROM THE AUTHOR[12]

These poems had been discarded, justly condemned by their character to oblivion, when old commitments obliged me to pull them out anxiously, quickly put them in order, and send them to the printer. I didn't really want to, to tell the truth, but there was no other solution; I was in dire straits. 'Go and good luck!' I told them, poor offspring of my grief. 'Among the living they now go, though they bear mortality and death.' They went without me knowing their destination or needing to.

It's been a decade—almost unimaginable given the speed of life today—since most were written, and the contradictions of my agitated life and faltering health did not let me refocus my tired eyes and flagging spirit on them. In re-reading, it was clear to me that they were incomplete and impoverished, and the manuscript lacked much to make it a work of value, instead of yet another book with no merit apart from a persistent melancholy that some will find, not unreasonably, tiring and monotonous. But some things are dictated by circumstance, and if I couldn't flee woe, no

---

[12] In what is not just an introduction, but a rhetorical posture staked out between the prejudices of her time and the poems, Rosalía de Castro reflects here not just on the provenance of the poems (which she doesn't tell the whole truth of; they were written over a longer period and in more places than Castile... and some had been published as well, making it easy for a reader to tell she is posturing), but on the condition of women and their relationship to thinking itself. When she claims women's role is lightness and their thought is frivolous, she is speaking slant; in the very first section of poems, 'Vagaries' (or 'Whimsies,' if you like, or 'Frivolities'), she makes clear that thinking *is* her business! For a fuller analysis of the structure of this part of the book, see Angueira 354-356.

wonder my poems couldn't. Written in the Castilian desert, in nature's solitude and in that of my heart, offspring of illness and absence, they reflect, perhaps too sincerely, the state of my spirits or, at times, my natural capacity (not for nothing am I a woman) for feeling the pain of others. Oh, sadness, muse of our time! It knows me well, and has for years; it sees me as its own, it's odd like me, does not leave me, not even when I wish to speak of other subjects currently in the air and in our hearts. Crazy me! In the air, did I say? In my heart, okay, but outside it, too? When is one person's experience ever that of others? Mine and everyone's! In my soul and in those of others! But that doesn't mean I think myself inspired, or that I think I've written a transcendental book. No, that was not my aim, nor do I think I have the strength for it. There are many serious things in the air, it's true; it's easy to be aware and talk of them; yet I'm a woman and, to women, it's as if our own feminine frailty allows us to perceive sorrows, feel them as they occur. We are harps of two strings, imagination and feeling; from the eternal honeycomb that we secrete in intimacy, all that emerges is honey, more or less sweet, more or less scented, but always honey, nothing more. If the problems occupying exalted minds concern us, it's when those who deal with them and bring their lifework to us can't hide their sorrows and failures! It's our job to see to their wounds, dress them, offer help and support, more with dumb acts than with words and murmurs. The thinking of women is light, just as butterflies fly from rose to rose pondering light things; the hard work of thinking is not for us. We unwittingly impregnate thinking with our innate debility; our frivolous or unaccustomed spirits easily stray, which doesn't happen to men of study and reflection, who realize that under the clear current of form there's naught in our thoughts but the insubstantial froth of vulgarities. And in speculative thinking such as that of art, there is nothing more useless or cruel than the vulgar. I've always fled from it with all my will, and to avoid such momentous sins I stick with simple poetry, though even there I sometimes encounter, in a felicitous expression or chance idea, a nameless force direct as an arrow that penetrates our flesh, makes us shudder, and resonates in the golden soul as a fellow being who, ouch!, answers the huge sigh that often rises in us in the face of earthly sorrow.

I add that this book does not stem from the inspiration that gave rise to *Galician Songs* or, at least, it doesn't seem so to me. That book of my days of hope and youth has a freshness proper to life beginning. Even if I tried, this new book, written amid upheavals, could not contain the enchanting innocence of first impressions: the sun of life that illuminates the world we inhabit doesn't shine at dawn in the same way that it glows at sunset, shrouded sadly in clouds of coming autumn.

Galicia was at the soul of *Songs*, while here it is more in the background. Yet just as only death can free the spirit from its shroud of flesh, even less can poets ignore where they live, and the natural world around them, ignore their times, and stop echoing, even unconsciously, the persistent lament that today is in every mouth. As such, though I can't say what in my book arises from my troubles, and what concerns those of others, I lay claim to them all, just as folks used to disappointment take on the suffering of others. In this new book, then, I chose, over compositions that might be personal, others that express the tribulations of the people who, one after another, and in different ways over time, suffered around me. There is so much hardship on this beloved Galician soil! Whole books could be written on the theme of the constant misfortune that afflicts villagers and mariners, the only real working people of this place. I've seen and felt their sorrows as if they were mine, but what always moved me, and which could not fail to echo in my poetry, were the innumerable worries of Galician women: beings who are loving with their own and with strangers, full of feeling, hardworking in body and gentle of heart, and at the same time so unfortunate that they say they were only born to prove how much exhaustion could afflict the weaker and frailer half of humanity. In the fields, they work alongside men doing heavy chores, while at home they bravely endure the worries of motherhood, householding, and arid poverty. Often alone, they work from sunrise to sunset and without help to keep themselves going, feed their children and perhaps a sickly parent; they appear condemned to find rest only in the tomb.

Emigration and military service continually take their lovers, brothers and husbands, depriving families of sustenance; abandoned and weeping, women spend their bitter lives in uncertain hope, dark loneliness and the anxiety of unrelenting poverty. The worst is that their men leave, some because they are taken away and others because example, necessity, and even at times a blind but forgiveable greed make them flee the cherished hearth where they are loved, leave spouses already mothers and their many children too young to realize, unlucky ones, that they are condemned to orphanhood.

When these poor martyrs dare to tell us their secrets, weep for their loves still living, or yearn in their sorrows, we discover in them such delicacy of feeling, such stores of tenderness (that the rest of their character is not enough to erode), and an abnegation so huge that we feel inferior to these unknown brave heroines who live and die doing marvellous things that go unnoticed, miracles of love and endless forgiveness. Their stories, worthy of being sung by poets in blessed harmony, can be expressed in a single note and chord, that of the sublime, and in the key of grief.

Though I lack ability, I tried to do this, above all in the poems of 'Widows of the Living, Widows of the Dead,' but I know I didn't succeed in saying what's needed. Though my forces are small, I wish I could sing all the truth and poetry of this epic, simple as it is painful.

Some will claim that I express myself in Galician because I speak of humble things. That's not the case. The multitudes in our countryside are unlikely to read these verses soon, verses written because of them, but only partly for them. What I wanted was to speak again of the problems of Galicia, in our own language, and repay in some way the appreciation and love that *Galician Songs* awakened in its enthusiasts. A book of two hundred pages written in the sweet dialect of our country was then something new, and traversed obstacles. Readers happily embraced it, and I understood that I had to make sure the first book wasn't the last. I couldn't rally people then desert the very flag I had raised.

So here are *New Leaves,* more aptly called old, and they're the last, for now I've paid my debt to my land, it would be hard to write more poems in my mother tongue. I offer you these poems, seeking not triumph but pardon, not praise but oblivion, with the mercy granted to bad books. It's time for the poems! Here's my desire: That the poems stream past like one more murmur, like the fragrance of countryside that bears poetry, born from vast solitudes, ever-green pastures and the stunning beaches of our seas, seeking a place in hearts that both suffer and love this beloved land, Galicia.

Rosalía de Castro
Santiago de Compostela, 30 March 1880

I

VAGARIES

I

Of women who write of doves and flowers,
it's said they've women's souls.
And me who doesn't write of them, oh Virgin of Paloma,[13]
    argh!! what soul have I??

---

[13] Here, in the opening poem, de Castro directly addresses the colonial centre, Madrid—where the Virgin of Paloma is revered and celebrated—to advise that she fully intends to be unruly, and to think.

II

I know well there's naught
that's new beneath the stars;
that others have thought already
things I think up now.

So then, why do I write?
So then, because that's what we are,
clocks that tick tick tick
perpetually going round.

III

        Just like clouds
        that wind impels,
and now they darken, now they hearken
the mighty spaiçes of the skies,
        so the wild
        ideas that I have,
images of many forms,
of strange making, of uncertain colours,
        now obscure,
        now clarify,
the bottomless depth of my thinking.

IV

You'll say of these lines, and it's true,
they've strange unsettled harmonies,
that in them ideas glow pale,
        like wandering embers
        which explose at times,
        which extinguish quickley,
that they ressemble the puff of soot
that whirls in the back garden,
and the monotone moan of the pines
        on savage shores.

I'll tell you that that's just how
my songs fly from my soul, in mayhem,
just as from deep oakwoods at first glint
        of day, emerges
        a buzz that no one can say
        if it's babble of breezes,
        if it's kíss of flowers,
these tangled, mysteryous harmonies
        that in this sad world
seek paths up to heaven , (lost)

V

New Leaves!! It makes me laugh,
this name you carry,
as if a dark one
overheard folk call her white.

Not *New Leaves* at all; a bundle
of gorse and thorns is all:
nettles, like my sorrows;
feral, like my grief.

Without scent or freshness,
savage regrets and wounds...
If in the scrubland you blossom,
who can blame you!!

VI

What's this buzz around me??
What's going on that I can't pin down?
I'm scared of what's
alive and can't be seen.
I fear the traitorous woe
that's coming, and where it arrives, no one knows.

VII

Some say: my land!
Say others: my darling!
And this: my memories!
And that: my friends!
All sigh, all,
for some lost treasure.
Only I don't say a thing,
only I never heave a sigh,
for my earthly body
and weary spirit
wherever I want to go,
        go with me.

VIII

        At night's apèx, there
in the light of the sad and waning lamp
or in black dreaded darkness,
            the old man sees phantoms.

Some are withered trees, and leafless:
           others, dried-up springs;
mountains eternally wrapt in snow,
           barrens that do not end.

        And at daybreak,
when with the last star they too dissolve,
others come, more sad and rancorous,
           for the bitter truth
they carry is scribbled in their lifeless eyes
           and on their bald crowns.

Never say, dear youth, you've lost the
           lilt of hope
that's always a friend as life begïns;
it's a mortal enemy only at the end!

IX

Peace, peace so craved;
for me, where is it??
Perhaps I'm not meant to...
Never had peaçe yet!!

Calm, rest,
where on earth are they?
In the aches that slay me,
in the grief they gïve me.

Peace, peace, you're a lie!
For me there's no p!

X

I once had a nail
nailed in my heart,
and I can't say now if that nail was
of gold, iron or love.
I only know that it pained me so deeply,
that it tormented me so much
that day and night I wept as constantely
as Magdelene at the Cross.
—Lord, gïven you can do all
I asked the Maker once,
—gïve me the pluck to pull the nail
out from where it lies.
And Gdd gave it me, and I pulled it free;
but... who'd have guessed? Afterward
I felt no more torment
nor did I know what pain was:
I only knew, I didn't know what I was missing
in the place where the nail'd been,
and prehaps, prehaps I felt nostalgic
for that ache.... Good Gwd!
This mortal clay that swaths the spírit
who can understand it, Lord![14]

---

[14] With Angueira and others, I call Rosalía a materialist poet, and 'a poet of loneliness, radically intimate and social loneliness, not of nostalgia.' (69) Though she was taken up by critics as a poet of nostalgia, of melancholy, a figure through which Galicia itself was written as melancholy and yearning, contemporary cultural critics in Galicia convincingly argue that Galicia as sentimental and melancholy is a construct built outside Galicia in order to weaken nationalism. Rosalía de Castro, in *New Leaves,* is so much more than 'melancholy'! Her arguments are material, focus on rights and justice, and don't shrink from portraying women's lives as oppressed by poverty, economic precarity, the clergy, marriage. To call her 'melancholy' is to vastly diminish her voice.

XI

When one's very joyful, very joyful,
        it's ridiculously arcane!,
almost as if, it seems a lie but isn't,
        joy comes as a burden.

As if deep deep in the entrails
        barren desert lies!
That never fills with laughter or contentments,
only with the fruits of bitter paiin!

        But when one has regrets
        and is truly unjoyed,
no hollow can be found in the wounded breast,
        grief so brims it!!

So bountiful is tribulation in its gifts,
that it pours them, thank the Maker!, till the apron overflows.
        Till the one who receives them,
        argh! bursts with surfeit.

XII

Today or tomorrow, who knows when?
        but mayb all too soon,
they'll come to wake me, and rather than one living,
        they'll find one dead.

All round me there'll arise
        grievous sobs,
cries of anguish, tearbursts of my children,
        of my precious orphan babes.

And I without heat, unmoving, cold,
        mute, unresponsive to it all,
that's how I'll be when death leaves me
        chilled by its breáth.

And farewell forever, to all I so loved!
        What dire abandon!
        Despite all the sarcasms
        there are, must be and ever were,
I never saw one to hush the living more
than the humble quietú d of a body deád.

XIII

    With no rancour or disdain,
nor with fear of change;
only thirst..., a thirst
for something I can't pin down, that slays me.
Rivers of life, where are you?
Air! I've got no air.

    —What d'you see in that deep dark?
What sight makes you tremble and go still?
—I don't see! I gaze as
do the blind in stárk sunlight.
And there I'll fall ,there where
what falls never rises. agáin,

XIV

That hum of song and laughter,
go, come, jostle loud;
that talk of what's gone by
and what has yet to be;
that impish vitality in short,
of the young, it hit me
hard, and I told them:
Get lost, don't return.

   Each by each they paraded quietly
every which way,
just as beads off a rosary
fall scattered on the ground.
And the patter of their steps, in leaving,
resounded inside me,
just as, no more sadly
will resound perhaps
in the depth of graves
the last farewell that the living bid the dead.

   At last I was alone, but so alone
that today the restless buzz of flies,
the rasping constnat gnaw of mouse,
and from the fire the snap
as from green wood
fresh sap is devoured,
all seems to speak to me, and I understand them,
they keep me company,

and my heart tells them trembling,
for Gawd's sake, don't go!

   How sweet too, but so sorrowful,
is solitude!

XV

    For each beat, another:
for one pain, another pained;
upon forgetting, another forgotten,
after love, love again.

    And at the end of such fatigue
and of such varied luck,
old age that grabs us by surprise
or the repose of death.

XVI

   When it was winter
I thought of where you'd be,
when it was sunny
I thought of where you'd head.
Now... I think only,
my love, what if you forget! (me)

XVII

   But see that my heart
is a centifolia rose,
and each petal is a sorrow
joined in life to another.

Pull one out, pull out two;
sorrows still I'll have to spare:
today ten, tomorr' forty,
as you pull that flower bare.

My heart you'll pull out then,
when no petals are there!

XVIII

With its deaföning and constant mormur
it lures me, the surf of this savage sea,
as the sirens lure when singing.
—In this bed of mine mysterious and cold,
it tells me, come softly and rest.

In love it is with me... the devil!
       and I in love with it.
We'll stay locked in stubborn battle,
for as much as the surf ceàselessly calls me, I'm
death-ly afraid to go lie there.

XIX

I go in search of honey and freshness
        to wet my dry lips,
and don't know how I find, nor where,
        burning and bitters.

I go in search of nectars to sweeten
        these biting stanzas of mine,
and don't know how, nor where, always
        fierceness finds them.

        As heaven and Creátor know,
        it's not my doing;
        argh! without wanting it, I've
a hurting sick heart.

XX
SILENCE!

Hand nervous and heart racing,
mists condensing in my eyes,
with a world of doubt in my senses
and a world of torment in my gut,
    feeling them struggle
    in unequalled battle,
immortal desires that torment
    and rancours that kill.
I soak the sharp quill in my own blood,
    bursting the swollen vein,
and I write...., I write...., why?? Go back
    to the dark pit of the soul,
    stórmy images!
Go abide with dead memories!
The hand trembling over the page writes only
words, and *words*, and *words*!
The form immaculate and pure of the idea,
    wherein it remained veiled?[15]

---

[15] An argument against purity in thinking. Here Rosalía de Castro has 'put an antic disposition on,' employing the deep sarcasm of *retranca* to reveal truths by saying the opposite. Without images or memory, of course, words *can't* unveil the idea. Her triple cry in the poem is Hamlet's, as is the poison and tumult. But whereas a whole play goes by before Hamlet's final words, 'The rest is silence,' RdC's 'SILENCE!' is where the *words, words, words* of her restless book (the poetics of the 'Vagaries' now done, ended with a veiled question) can begin.

II

INTIMACIES

FAREWELL![16]

Farewell, hills and meadows, chapels and bells;
farewell, Sar and Sarela rivers, rife with brambles;
Farewell, glad Vidán, mills and gorges;
Conxo, of sombre cloister and placid fallow fields;
San Lourenzo hiding, like a child in the bushes;
Belvis, place for me of fondest memories;
San Domingos where I went in need of rest;
lives of my life, part of my very core.
And you, too, shadowed lonely walls
who've seen me weep alone and broken;
farewell, dear shadows! Farewell, detested shades!
    Once again, fortune's reverses
        drag me far away.

On my return, if I come back, all'll still be where it was;
the same dark hills and the same dawns
gazing into the waters of Sar and Sarela,
the same green fields, the same dark steeples
of the stern cathredal eyeing the horizons.
But those whom I now leave as gentle springs
or in the green of life, without outbursts or tears,
when I be back, how far will they, impelled by change,
have tread along misfortune's way?
As for me..., there's nothing in the world I dread
        but the long wait for death!

---

[16] Rosalía names rivers or neighbourhoods in and around the bustling and beloved capital of Santiago de Compostela, a place she left in 1879 when her family moved to Lestrove, nearby. It's delightful that her 'intimacies' are not just inside the self, but outside, in her surroundings. The first poem of this section of the book is a reversal of what we think of as 'intimacy.' By starting with this reversal, Rosalía underscores the importance of place and surroundings to the sense of self. *Cathredal*, Rosalía's spelling of 'cathedral,' reflects the popular pronunciation of the word, and I maintain this spelling: the Cathredal as theatre, as catheatral.

*

    Field crickets, mole crickets, pale wee cicadas,
Toads and insects of every hue,
while in the distance, cart axles are singing,
what loving serenades
they always gïve us from the fields!

      Just in remembering them,
      I don't know what it does to me,
        don't know if it's good
        don't know if it's bad.

*

How the clouds in open space
    flit and wánder!
    Some are white,
    others are black;
Some seem to me as doves puffed round,
    others dispatch
    leggy light....

Divergent winds blow in the heights,
    twirl in all directions,
they púsh the clouds without order or rudder,
    don't ask me where
    and I don't know why.

They lift clouds away, just as years lift off
    our dreams,
    and our very hope.

*

   Rich or poor, back then
all tarried, so content and calm!
Now poor or rich, gone to the dêvil,
     everything, all of it lost!

   Days pass unbidden, years slip by,
     and even centuries wíll fly.
Though abundant springs go dry,
there's others too that flow forever;
but the springs perennial in this life
     are always toxic.

   In them, the spirit that pines with hurt,
bathes in the sickly damp of rancour,
     unable to
sip forgetfulness of waters that cure.

   Hate's a hellish progeny!
Love can put an end to it; but you,
memorie, keep recalling every slight.
     Yes, you! You're cause of ill!

IN THE CATHREDAL

Every day, in every recess
of the vaste temple,
old folks, nodding off,
mutter Aves and Pater Nosters;
and the archbishops in their tombs,
kings and queens, incredibly calm
in the peace of marble, sleep in tranquillity
while clerics sing in the choir.
The organ swells in sad clamours,
those of the bells, far off, answer,
and the holy image of the Redeemer
appears to sweat blood in the grotto.

Holiest Lord, at your feet,
I too sweat beads of anguish!
But if you always punish sin,
give help to the afflicted one
   who asks.

Sunset, through the stained glass image
of our Lady of Solitude, emanates serene
rays, that dress angels and the Eternal Father
in hues of glory.
Saints and apostles—look! their lips
seem to move, to speak quietly
to each other, and up in the heights
of heaven, the music is about to start
as those in the greát orchestra
tune their joyful instruments.

Will they come alive? Will they stay stone,
those countenances so realistic,
those marvellous tunics,
those eyes full of life?
You who made them with the help of the Maker,
you with the immortal name, Master Mateo,
from there where you humbly rest
kneeling, tell me.
But you, curly-headed one, when
we touch your saintly head to ours, are silent... so I pray.[17]

Here Glory reigns, but there,
in that bláckened arcade lies hell
and the sad souls of the damned,
there where every demon gnaws them.
I can't stop staring,
half astonished, half in fear,
for all of them seem to me
a delirium of mortal spectres.

How they gaze at me, those corpses
   and those demons!
How they fix on me, mocking
from the columns where they were set!
Are they real? Or not?
  Saints of heaven,
will they recognize me as one
   they've seen before?
So órphaned, so grieving,
but as numb as they are...

---

[17] RdC refers here to the 'santo dos croques,' a kneeling stone statue of a curly-haired boy-man with whom visitors traditionally bump heads upon entering the Cathedral, so as to transfer wisdom from the stone head to their own. It is said to be the image of Master Mateo, architect of the cathedral.

How they afíx on me...! I'm going, yes, going,
   I'm so afraid!

   But already in the prisms of the chandelier
      falls the final
quiet ray that afternoon sun
      serenely lays down:
and in each pretty pendant of the candelabra
      lively reflections,
scintillating like stars,
paint a thousand hues upon the floor,
and make the ghostly dust specks
seem miracles, appear portents.
   But then come shadows suddenly...
All darkens, inscrutable...
Farewell, dark pearls and marvels....
Behind Mount Pedroso, Phoebus sets.

   While the phantoms wander in the naves,
whispering Aves and Pater Nosters,
old folks ask God for
help only he can gìve.
For when world shakes us off, it's only then
that we anxiously seek heaven.

   At the feet of Our Lady of Solitude,
we've kept company for many years!,
I prayed the prayer I've always prayed,
remembering my secrets,
for my mother I leave caresses,
for my children kísses, thousands;
for the tormenters of my spirit
I prayed... and left, I was so afraid.

*

   Race on, serene and crystal waves,
head out majestically in calm, as do
the shades of glorious deeds!
Roll past, relentless, as roll
countless generations to eternity
who've contemplated you just as I do!
Gïve me your perfume, pretty roses;
to my thirst that burns, may clear fountains
quench its fire; clouds of mist,
protect me with your veil of delicate lace
from glaring rays of ardent sun;
and you, soft touch of breeze,
strike up mysterious concerts
amidst the oaks at the dark edge of pastures
past which the Sar flows, murmuring softly.

   Time flees quickly; perhaps even lightning
falls more slowly across the immensity of space
than do the years in passing.
For me, they race past in fierce battle...
and have raced by me just the same... and day arrives...!
Gïve me your kísses and open your arms to me
here by the river, in meadow-fresh grasses...
Don't tell anyone where I am...; in flowers
which I wish would hide
my telltale wound...., may my body never feel the touch
of profane hands to lift me yónder...
I want to stay where my griefs abide!

*

Every night I pondered tearful...
hoping vast night would not stay,
and yet it lasts... and lasts... in its midst
  may the night of sorrow
  enfold my keening...

But the insolent light of day,
  steady in its betrayal,
  each and every dawn
has penetrated radiant with glory
right to the bed where I lay stricken
  with my afflictions.

Ever since, I seek night
  deep and dark,
and I crave darkness in vain, for always
night's sweep ends with dawn...
Only inside me, seeking darkness
  and entering shadows,
a night has arrived that is unending:
  in my stricken soul.

YESTERDAY YOU, TOMORROW ME

    I fell so low, so low,
light cannot reach me;
I've lost sight of stars
and abide in darkness.

    But wait...! Why do you laugh,
insensitive to my struggle!
I'm still alive..., I can still
rise to take revenge.

    Casting stones at one who's fallen,
Go ahead and cast a hundred,
cast, and when you all stumble,
they'll do the same to each of you.

*

   May this cup from which you drink
     life's sweetness,
bear a drop of gall, just one,
squeezed from my aching heart.
   You'll understand then
how paine softens cold stones,
    though it can't soften
iron souls and vicious hearts.

GOOD LOVES

    Like the scent of roses that rises from the branches
on a morning in May, there are gentle loves
felt as they arrive, though they enter unseen
through the cherished door that the heart opens them
        willingly, as in August
        the flower opens in afternoon mist.
    And without murmur or complaint, or tears, or tune,
soft and wistful, like the breath of angels,
they incarnate purely in us, move in our blood
and turn the barrens green in spirit wherever they abide.
        Seek these loves, seek them,
          if you have one who can gïve you love,
        for these loves are all that's lasting
        in this fleeting life.

MEAN LOVES

     It was ache and cholera,
    was fear and aversion,
    was a love lopsided,
    a castigation from Above!
  There are dark loves, that weigh heavily,
that deprive spirits, that cloud consciences,
that bite when they caress, that burn with their gaze,
that gïve angry pain, that stain and confront.
     Better to die of cóld
     than warm yourself at their hearth.

*

      Open wide, new roses:
      gleam, carnations:
trees, dress yourselves in your garden
      in pretty leaves of green.
Vines that once lent us shade,
      come to cover us again with amazements.
      Beautiful nature,
      eternally the same,
tell all mortals, tell again those driven mad
they'll also perish!

NO CHARGE...

When they tuck the shroud around me
    if I bear one;
when they lay me in the coffin
    if I have one;
when they intone the responses,
if there's wherewithal to pay the clergy,
and when down in the grave....
Even if Saint Peter pulls me out,
I can't help laughing
like the devil just think-ing of it!
What a burial, for they have to put me in the ground
even if no one pays them...!

WHO WOULDN'T SIGH...

    Light and progress everywhere..., but
        doubts still linger,
and tears come and who knows why,
and griefs seem to have no reason.

    Same old tune! they say, tired
of this chorus, they who keep on arriving, leave
in new batches, and wander blindly
        seeking what doesn't exist.

    Reprobates!... Always probing in the dark
        which mutely tells you nothing.
Seek faith, which was lost in doubt,
        and quit your sighing.

    But they, too, lost,
head up one path and down another,
with no idea, suckers! where they go,
        without peace, direction, without faith.

. . . .
    Sad's the song we're singing.
But what if there's no better song?
    Greát light blinds the eyes,
and greát desire makes us anxious.
      When plagues befall us
        one after another, we can't do more
        than hurriedly bury our dead,
        duck our heads, and hope
the waves of sickness pass us by...
      Pass by!... for others will come.

*

   They howled at me as I walked on,
      nearly exhausted,
without energy but deep in thought
and with the fatal poison I carried.
    And those whose paths I crossed,
      on seeing me struggle,
in my pain and my affront,
      the turncoats mocked me
(and did so as soon as they guessed).
    —If it knew my pain, dear God,
I thought trembling, even the current
      of the river would turn against me.

  Seeking shelter of the highest walls,
      on deserted roadways,
bloodying my feet on sharp gravel,
I was nearly at the place I loved,
imagining with excitement: —Will my babes
      be awake already?
Oh, if they see me arrive so battered,
tearful, breathless and bleeding,
they'll be so shaken, my poor babies,
      at seeing their unlucky mother!

    Little by little I went on,
and climbed the stairs in fear,
my sad heart leaping:

I listened! Not even the buzz of flies.
In the cradle my angels still slept,
> protected by the Virgin Mother.[18]

---

[18] The destitution of women rings loud here, the economic struggle that requires them to leave the home. In darkness, what could it be that this woman needs to do, that would take her away from her children? Even today, we can read in this poem an intimation of the many ways in which women are never out of danger, and have to take risks with their bodies to make a living.

*

Why, sweet soul of mine,
why do you not want now
what you once wanted?

Why, thoughts,
why do you not thrive now
upon desires you love?

Why, my spirit,
why do you now feel humiliated,
when once you were proud?

Why, heart,
why do you not speak now
sweet words of love?

Why do you no longer throb
with the soft pulse
that calms all worry?

Why, finally, my Maker,
have I so long been without
earth and heaven?

And you! rósy star
that they say was born
with me, you might as well

   Go dim forever,
since you weren't even able
to forever light my way!

THE PEAL OF DAWN

     Cathredal bell
    grave, sad and sonorous,
    when, at the glimmer of day
    you peal the peal of dawn
    in silent space,
    resounding melancholy;
    your striking chimes
awaken feelings I barely recall.

     Some were pure
    as the glow of dawn,
    others like the hope
    which lovers dream,
    and the last were restless,
    half light, half shadow,
    half a pleasure without name,
and half a dread surprise.

     Oh! how years have run by
    and dawns passed,
    and luck worn thin,
    and worries risen.
    Now when you resound, bell,
    when you strike the stroke of dawn,
    My eyes brim and I break
into quiet tears.

    How müted and sad,
    how fearfully you echo
    in my waiting ear,
    messenger of the dawn
    when at daybreak
    you solemnly toll....!
    Where did
fortune and glory, once awakened, go?

    They're gone forever;
    but you, grave and sonorous,
    oh, at the break of day,
    with your melancholy voice
    you daily see and show us
    every nascent dawn;
    and it seems that death's knell,
theirs and mine, is what you toll.

    Cathredal bell,
    so grave and so sonorous,
    why do you keep sounding
    each candid dawn
so that I must hear you
and dissolve in tears?
But very soon..., very soon, my ears
will not hear you in evening, or at dawn.

*

   Sea! with your fathomless waters;
sky! with your immensity;
help me to bury the phantasm
that terrorizes me.

   It's bigger than you all,
and extends further...
with one foot where the stars gleam,
and the other where they dig my grave.

   Implacable cruel trickster,
it's always just ahead of me,
and threatens to pursue me
even to eternity.

*

>Dig quickly, dig down,
>>looming thoughts,
>dig a deep hole where we'll bury
>>all memory of the past.
>>Lay the dead in the ground!
>>Dig, dig quickly!
>And for tombstone you'll offer dark forgetting,
>and no place, for sacred ground.

*

When I think you've gone,
black cloud that clouds me,
at the base of my pillow
you turn to mock me.

When I think you've left,
even in the sun you show up,
and you're the star that shines,
and are the wind that moans.

If there's song, it's you who sings,
if tears, it's you who crys them,
and you are the river murmur
and are the night and are the dawn.

You are in all and you are all,
for me and even in me you abide,
nor will you ever let me go,
cloud that always clouds me. [19]

---

[19] In Galician, where verbs do not need pronouns except in cases of emphatic speech or to remove ambiguity, the word 'I' is missing in the lines 'When I think...' and 'When I imagine...' This is a poem of deepest intimacy, in which the self-reflexive self, the I, is unpronounceable and untouched, and yet is so profoundly touched it cannot arise: this paradox is both the dark struggle of depressive illness and the struggle of a nation unacknowledged and denied autonomy. For Galicians, this poem resonates as a national anthem; it's been put to music, sung by the greatest voices; once heard, you hear it forever. As Angueira and de Cebreiro insist, the poem is radically contemporary in its structure and evocation. It could also be versioned this way in English, without the I, and maybe both versions need to be present!

In thinking you've gone,
black cloud that clouds me,
at the base of my pillow
you turn to mock me.

In thinking you've left,
even in the sun you show up,
and you're the star that shines,
and are the wind that moans.

If there's song, it's you who sings,
if tears, it's you who crys them,
and you are the river murmur
and are the night and are the dawn.

You are in all and you are all,
for me and even in me you abide,
nor will you ever let me go,
cloud that always clouds me.

LUCK BETRAYS

      Tremble if a stroke of greát luck
      catches you on this earth by surprise;
      superhuman glories, here,
      bring supreme misadventures.
Don't even think that hurt will pass
as whims do on this earth;
      there are hells in memory,
      even when the conscience is clear!

As ivy roots across high walls,
in some hearts, aches take root,
      and some of them undermine life
      as ivy roots do stone.
      Yes; tremble when on this earth
      you feel huge luck:
      its better that your life flows
      as do serenity's waaters.

*

    Lead me to that clear fountain
        where together we sip
the purest waters that quench
the thirst of love and the flame of desire.
Lead me by the hand as you once did...
        But no, I fear
        I'll see in its clear liquid
        the shadow of the dark
disappointment without cure or consolation
        that time's lodged between us.

AT THE MANOR OF A...

     Late afternoon it was,
the trill of the crickets areády rising,
     water roared loudly over the dam,
and fugitive fires flickered distant.
  Below the mountain, the chérished manor
stood majestic in the darkening village,
     with the ancient olive
as curtain for its window.
     The staircase was deserted,
     the paternal nest stood empty,
and over it, falling mysteriously
in the dusky shadow, was oblivion.

     Who looks to the past
     with compassionate gaze?
     Who recalls the dead,
when even the living can't remember?

*

   In the skies, blue so clear;
on the ground, green intensity;
in the depth of my soul,
all's sombre and dark.
   What joyful procession!
What laughter and ease!
And my eyes even so
are full of tears.
   Swathed in green,
the fields gleam afresh,
while bitter gall
settles in my heart.

THE HAND OF JUSTICE

Those known as honourable in town,
stole from me my every brightness,
cast muck on my finery in a single day,
and threw me an old smock in tatters.
They left not a stone where I'd lived;
homeless, without abode, I lived amid potatoes;
slept rough in the meadows with hares;
my children... my angels!! whom I so loved,
they died, died for hunger killed them!
I was dishonoured, they tarnished my life,
left me a bed of thorn and bramble;
while they, malicious weasels,
slept calmly in a bed of roses.

—*Save me, oh judges!* I yelled... Crazy hope:
they mocked me, and justice sold me out.
—*God, help me God!* I cried, and yelled again...
but from on high, no deity heárd me.
That's why, like any hurt or wounded she-wolf,
in a raging lunge I grabbed the sickle,
swung slowly... Not even grass felt it!
And the moon hid, and the wild beast slept
with her companions in a feather bed.

I watched them calmly, and raised my hands,
with a whack, just one! I left them lifeless.
And satisfied, I sat beside the victims,
quiet, waiting for day to dawn.

And so..., so justice prevailed:
I, on them; and the laws, on the hand that smote them.[20]

---

[20] It is notable that, for Rosalía, this too is an intimate poem. Revolution is intimate!

*

   God's cast a veil over
our very hearts,
veil that hides abysses
only he can view.
   When I think of what they'd see,
as I bow in adoration
humble, on my knees
as one does to adore the Lord,
if this veil between the two
were suddenly to slip;
I tremble... and bowing lower
say: —how wise God is!

*

Tick-tock, tick-tock! In night's silence
the pendulum repeates its sinister beat,
while the whetted arrow
that times each instant amid shadows,
on the ever immobile clock-face
slowly points across its limpid sphere.
All below is darkness
and only in the immense heights,
in the sky's limitless breadth
some restless star glows
just as, in the ash after a spring burn,
the last sparks gleam in the cinders.
And the pendulum's beat surges
as a heart beats when filled with ache;
it resonates fearfully
in thick darkness.
In vain the fearful eye wanders
in the dark;
one silent instant after another
passes, and others arrive silently
in their wake, falling into eternity
as grain does upon the grindstone;
without the future, veiled from mortal eyes,
breáking through the heavy mist.

How sad night is, and the clock sad too,
as body and conscience keep restless watch!

OLD FRIENDS

   When amid the triste and chilly naves
      between high walls,
how cold they are, how sad,
when in the evening I go to pray,
what crazy and strange thoughts
come and go in my head!

   Deafening silence I know so well,
it's been my friend all these years,
full of many memories,
and while the spirit seems to hear
      its mortal echo,
in the greát basilica's spaces
silence reigns with mysterious serenity.

   Quavering shadows, tremouring rays,
      by the altar
they settle, wander, flee and loom
      forward and back.
And the holy Apostle, seated as ever
      on his dais
of silver and gold, stiffly contemplates
all that's there, with staring eyes.

  If only I were saint, were stone
      of the kind found here,
like St. Peter, holding his keys,
or John the Baptist, one finger held high,
I would've seen generations pass
      one after another,

without fear of life and its torments,
without fear of death that shakes us.

   Soon our sad pilgrimage
       draws to a close.
People pass on, like clouds
       of summer.
And stones remain... , and when I'll die,
       you, cathredal,
you, dark hulk, heavy and morose,
when I'm no more, you'll still be.

*

   In the sway of May, long May,
All is draped in roses;
for some, they dress the dead,
for others, marriage poses.
   In the sway of May, long May,
you held but short sway óver me;
with you came my gaiety,
with you, it turned to flee.

FADED MOON

    Moon faded
to the hue of pale gold,
you see me and I don't want you
to see me, from so high.
As you're crossing space,
lift me quietly on your rays.

    Star to orphan souls,
    faded moon,
    I know well you won't light
    sadness such as mine.
    Go tell your Maker
and ask him to lift me up where he bides.

    But you tell him nothing,
    faded moon,
    and not in this world nor
    in another, will I find fortune.
    If you know where death
    tends its dark abode,
then ask death to lift my body and soul together
to where no one will remember,
not in the world where I am, nor in the heights above.

*

  How placidly they glow
river, fountain, and sun!
How they shine..., but their shine is not
     for me, no.

  How they flourish, grass and bushes
how the buds flower in the trees!
But their flourishing or flowering is not
     for me, no.

  How they sing, the birds
their amorous songs!
but though they sing, their song is not
     for me, no.

  How beautiful Nature
smiles at May's caress!
But the smile is not
     for me, no.

  Yes... for all there's bits of
air, light, warmth...
But in this *some for all* there's none
     for me, no.

  And so!... since in this place I find no
air, no light, no soil nor sun,
will there not be a tomb for me?
     For me, no.

STRANGER IN HER OWN LAND

     By the worn veranda
grizzled with ivy and lilies
she went to sit quietly and sadly
     across from the old chapel.

     The interminable procession of the Dead,
some still embodied, some in spirit,
slowly appeared upon the crest
     of the straight road,
glowing steady and pale,
like clothes hung above a lawn.

She contemplated how they passed and passed,
     filing on together to infinity,
     without gazing upón her
with their dull and sunken eyes
     that gave no sign or hint
of once having known her.

  And some were her lovers in the past,
some were family, and others friends,
childhood playmates,
servants and neighbours.
But passing and passing in front of her,
the dead just pressed forward
walking indifferently
the road of infinity,
while the silent night drew close
its sad bereavements

around a stranger in her own land,
who, without abode or ally,
sat on the veranda watching
how their fleeting flickers glówed.

*

> *Padrón...! Padrón...!*
> *Santa María... Lestrove...*
> *Farewell! Farewell!*

I

That laughter unending,
that frolic without pain,
that crazy happiness,
    why did it end?
Those sweet melodies,
those loving murmurs,
those serene nights,
    why are they gone?
The sonorous quiver
of harp strings and the sounds
of wistful guitar,
    who took them?
Everywhere mute silence,
    loneliness, ache,
where once luck itself
    reigned alone...

> *Padrón...! Padrón...!*
> *Santa María... Lestrove...*
> *Farewell! Farewell!*

II

    The Adina cemetery
is enchanting, it's true,
with its dark olive trees
ever fondly recalled;
with its carpet of grasses and
flowers, pretty as any God's made;
with its retired clerics
sitting outside to take the sun;
with children who play there
ebullient and glád;
with pale flagstones laid down,
and with a damp heap
of earth, where some poor soul
was interred at dawn.
    Long have I loved you,
enchanting simetery,
with your dark olives
older than my grandparents;
with your venerable priests,
who sit out in the sun
while birds raise in chorus
their matinal refrains,
and with your ossuary, humble
yet imposing respect
when the light that burns in it
shines resplendent at night.
I've loved you greátly and still do,
even the Maker knows this is true;
but today, thinking of you
my heart clouds over,
for the earth is upturned,
    dark, bereft of flower.

Padrón...! Padrón...!
Santa María... Lestrove...
Farewell! Farewell!

III

   I went one day to seek them,
heart pounding aloud,
I went calling each one
and none gave reply.
   I knocked at one door then another,
sensed no speech or voice
and as if in an empty tomb
my knock echoed.
   I looked through the lock,
what silense...! what fear...!
saw but wandering shadows
that passed without sound,
like wisps that float upward
in a ray of bright sun.
   My hair stood on end
from eerieness and grief.
Not one...! not any...!
Where are they? What became of them?
   The sad sound of the bell
slowly reached me...
Death had taken them, it pealed!

Padrón...! Padrón...!
Santa María... Lestrove...
Farewell! Farewell!

KEEP GOING...

    Shine, ray of dawn,
in a dream of peace clear and bright.
To one born blind, what does
      your divine blaze matter?

    Sigh, serene waves,
      as winds moan through the pines.
Music, oh! and songs and harmonies,
      to the deaf, what good are they?

    Keep going, pass by, you beauties,
you cure all who hope and love.
Loves and pleasures, though, are just a lie
      to those with parched souls.

*

     Why, God of pity
     why do they call it crime
to seek the death so long in coming,
     when a person's life
     exhausts and afflicts her?

     Heavy with sorrows,
     what heart can resist?
What tired traveller does not crave
     to seek the rest
     theyir body begs for?

     Why if one can't quell
     the hurts that oppress,
why's it said you'll be angry
     if such a person bows low
     into the tomb?

     Hell on earth
     and unending hell
beyond the deep pit of the grave,
     that the soul covets,
     and that eyes can't gauge.

     If it's that this is really true,
     and it's terrible truth!,
either you grant lonely hell
     to the many who keep enduring,
or if not that, holy Maker, pity the sad!

SHE'S ALONE!

   Clear were the days,
laughing the mornings,
and yet her own sadness
dark as orphanhood.
   She came at dawn's light,
returned at evening's...;
but whether she came or went
no one sought to know.
   One daylight she took
the path along the dunes...
As no one awaited her,
she returned no more.
   Three days passed before
the sea released her,
and there where the crow rests,
she lies interred alone.[21]

---

[21] This sequence of poems, in which each poem has reached to touch death's proximity and death's distance, in relation to the person and to the socius, draws to a close. Here Rosalía again articulates the loneliness of sadness, in a world that is in itself not sad—for the natural world enlivens our mundane one always—but in which affliction and precarity are constant. The fathomless sea is also the impossibility of comprehending death. The theological interdiction against suicide, railed at in the previous poem, is here faced with a woman's suicide quietly achieved, ending the book of intimacies.

III

VARIETIES

OF ANY CURSE, THERE'S NO WORSE
(THAN HEARTBREAK)

I

—Sweet Mariana, get thee to the river.
—I beg, my mother, that here I may stay,
that I not see the light of day,
that light itself not see me.
—What's this you're saying, girl...?
—That yesterday morning in the meadow
the water turned red
when I went to bathe there;
and below my foots
it was staining grasses:
that the sun in hitting my face
turned me a waxen colour;
and the shells of chestnuts
tangled in my hair;
the thorns of thornbushes
savagely attacked me;
in going down the paths
brambles snagged me;
nettles stung me;
dunes startled me,
and wee birds in seeing me
intoned a mournful plaint:
Sweet Mariana's going to die...!
Everyone, pray for her!

    —Oh, our Lady of Carme,
my daughter is ill!
Oh, God, they've cursed her!
Argh, a witch blew foul on her!
If you weren't so pretty,
no one would envy you.
Gïft of my own womb,
come to me, don't worry,
go ask help of St. Peter the Martyr,
he does more than sell bulls and cows...
—Loving mother, my mother,
you can bring me where you wish,
but for me there's no cure
anywhere on earth,
for it's just that a heart
holds me in chains,
and it's just that a foul mouth
has cursed me badly...

    —Who cursed you, my daughter?
What evil, sweet child, did you dö?
—Don't even ask, my mother,
it's best you not know.
The secrets of this curse
are best left sleeping under stones.
—Speak, girl, I feel
the blood boil in my veins.
—Better had I not seen light of day
that light'd never seen me...
Loving mother, dear mother,
don't curse me as did the witch.
Let me go with my secraet
to sleep deep in the ground.

—You'll not go with your secraet;
you'll not go, though you wish;
your mother will follow you asking
and there you'll answer.
—Oh, my mother! He was pretty
as angels are in churches,
his loving murmurs
far, far smoother than silk;
he was sweet... much sweeter
than honey from the comb.
He smelled of May roses,
his eyes were stars,
and like pure gold were
his curly locks...
—Stop, Mariana, stop,
my heart is breaking...
Who is this? tell me, tell me...
Or maybe it was a dream, my girl?
—It was no dream, Mama, I do not dream,
though I really wish I did.
I dallied with the count, my lady,
the countess's betrothed.
He spoke to me in the oaks
when I was gathering firewood;
he spoke to me at the river
on serene summer evenings;
I talked to him..., oh I'd talk
Mom dear, for the rest of my life!
—Oh dear blessed Virgin,
my daughter's taken ill,
ill with heartbreák
that did her very honour ill.
No wonder the birds sang to you,
dear Mariana, my treasure:

Sweet Mariana's going to die!
Pray for her, everyone!

   Sweet Mariana withers,
the poor girl's gone pallid,
she's touched no food,
no waater she wishes.
Friends cannot console her,
no music cheers her,
at the sight of sun she wheezes
at the sight of flowers she shakes.
Her mother's going crazy
seeking healing herbs,
which she places nightly
on Mariana's pillow,
and she goes to every hermitage,
with offering upon offering
to every blessed Virgin,
to all the saints, she prays
and lights candles in the niches
so the dead will intercede.
But Mariana does not recover,
Mariana still lies pale...
All say that a vampire
comes in the dark to suck her blood,
some say they've seen at night
souls wandering in the village.

II

   —Your lovestruck girl is dying from what?
Because of me, the beauty's dying?

Never! For it's unbefitting
to my very nobility.
Dry up those tears,
stop crying, old woman,
that girl of flowing tresses
will soon be my countess.
We'll go now to tell her,
we'll go together to her side.
 And off they set at a fine trot
through the meadow.

—Oh Sire..., don't you hear crows?
They're heading from the village...
Look at their wings beat...
just as black wings do.
—Let wings beat, crows
shów off like that when flying.
—Sire, sire..., how they caw!
Their caw augurs something!
It's that they foretell death,
there's death here nearby.
—Perhaps! May God embrace
the one who takes leave of earth.
—Oh Sire, they're tolling death...
Oh! it's our own churchbell ringing...
My Virgin! Who'd be dying?
—Don't think about who'll die,
old girl, think only
of your daughter ailing.
—Sire, sire..., we've far to go;
lay on the lash, for god's sake,
for when I left, at dawn's brink,
none lay ailing in the village

but my daughter,
who had the colour of earth,
and feet like cold snow,
and tiny hands like wax,
and all around her sad eyes
something like dark circles.
—You scare me with your words,
and impatience assails me...
I'd gïve half my lands
to save her life:
the most beautiful village girl
there is in all the region.
If it's that we find her dead,
if that's what we'll be finding...
If she dies, until my death
I must do penance.

   She died, did Mariana;
the count saw her between lit tapers,
but she did not see him;
she'd died before he came.
She died just like a little bird,
and in the shroud that holds her
she's like an ángel who awaits
for heaven to come for her.
. . . .
. . . .
   No one knew she'd died from love
and from being forgotten;
some said a plague
had sent her to her tomb;

others said it was a witch
who blew a foul stink on her...
But for her, the count did
penance till his life's end.[22]

---

[22] To open the variousness of this book of varieties, Rosalía reworks a tale from the tradition of popular oral romance, 'Mariana and the Count of Andrade,' collected (and already manipulated) by her husband, Manuel Murguía. Its appeal lies clearly in the effect on women of differences in class in matters of love. It is, thus, an economic poem, and a poem of voices, for many of the various poems play on voices. The influence of Rosalía de Castro's workings out of popular culture is visible in contemporary Galician literature as well, as in the works of Chus Pato, for example, and in all Pato's voices and dialogues in her poems.

TIME TO GET DRINKING

—I've three white hens
    and one black rooster,
gonna lay good eggs
    when the time comes;
gonna sell them high
    in January;
gonna save the moolah
    for a pretty mantilla;
gonna dress in it
    at my wedding;
gonna...

—Hey, there, Marica
    go fetch a pint,
and don't take off
    those rags for now,
let the hens hang out
    with the black rooster,
so they lay their eggs,
    and never mind that guff
about January, moolah
    and weddings,
love o' my life,
    it's time to get drinking![23]

---

[23] A poem of the economics of marriage in emigration's absence, and its effect on women. Marica, figure of fun in popular rhyme, is recuperated here by Rosalía to create a refraction. In telling the story without comment, the status of women *in* marriage is made clear... as it is in the next two poems as well, *before* marriage.

*

—A true love is greát and blessed,
     delight of all delights,
and it's sweet... sweeter than all sweetness.
     —Perhaps that's why, so often,
one way or another,
it brings 'heartburn,' as everyone knows.
     —But if it ends with a wedding?
     —Even if in a wedding it ends;
love's just like any dessert, my dear,
     as everyone knows
     like they know fire burns,
the more you take in, the more you regret it later.

*

    —Don't sing, don't cry, don't laugh, don't talk,
don't enter, don't leave without my permission.
In the name of St. Peter, just gïve me some room!
    —Well that's how it is, child, don't be cranky,
for if you sing, cry, laugh, and talk...
Who let the dog out? they'll soon say of you, girl.

ALERT!

   In spooky darkness
and the raucous murmur of wild pines
that the storm tosses and enslaves,
there was heard, as if a fox's yelp,
a fearful whistle.

   A dread lament to make blood run cold
answered the fearful whistel,
from deep in the thicket,
escalating the sadness the spirit feels
at the hoarse murmur of the border river.

   Between dark banks gentle and slow,
just as resigned thoughts flow
between sad remorse and hope,
wind came like a compass needle
racing from the furthest reaches.

   But at the edge of the wide bank,
mysterious and crouched, a sentinel
in a Miño skiff was resting;
with gun in hand and wakeful,
through the branches he kept watch.

NOT IN THE DARK!

I

—All's dark, shadows couch the pathway,
and not even heaven has eyes, nor pine woods tongues.

Let's go! Who knows the depth of what's hidden?
There's no soul who knows! Come! Night's dark.

—Dark? But there's a glow of some treacherous light...
—It's a star that glows in roiling waters.

—And don't you hear something rustle in the grass?
—It's the wind gone crazy, twirling foliage.

—Listen, I feel footsteps, and some shape hulks there...
—If it's alive, we'll kill it; it won't talk if it's dead!

—But here, by this headland, there's a deep hole:
come on, and saint or devil, we'll see what finds us there.

II

And where'm I heading? Where'll I hide?
So that no one sees me and I see no one.

The light of day startles me, starlight astonishes me.
And men's stares penetrate my very soul.

And it's that whatever is inside me, can be seen
on my face, just as tides deliver up their dead, at last.

If it be so, then let it be seen....! but no: I bear you
inside me: terrifying phantasm of my remorse! [24]

---

[24] This two-part poem and the preceding one make a diptych. In the first poem the scene is described from outside, and we see but the shadow of the border guard along the Miño (the river that forms the border between Galicia and Portugal) and of his gun, signifying his readiness to kill. In the two-part second poem, the dialogue of the fleeing couple in the first part is taken up in the second part by the woman's frightened voice alone; the man's voice is absent. The poems work eerily together; we too are in the dark. Is the man dead and the woman found?

*

    Immense elms, myrtles
that flaunt white flowers,
some still just budding,
others wind-plucked of petals,
boxwoods already centuries old
that go green together,
their branches and trunks forming
walls no one can penetrate,
in which tired serpents make
burrows in which to nest.
Bay trees, kin of boxwoods
in height and in origin,
now rooted timeless
deep in the earth.
Lemon and orange trees
that green moss shades
spread the scent of their blossoms
which reinvigorates us all.
Eternal forests in which
mysterious shadows reign,
crossed only by birds
down sad leafy lanes
where the murmur of springs
sounds almost like a plaint,
and where summer's sun
penetrates with melancholy.
And in the midst of this thicket
and this beautiful sadness,
in a house even sadder still,
but with proud façade,

there they say is the nest
of the mother of all witches:
house with cedar doors,
grilles in each window,
kitchen vast as those of monks,
silence as in churches,
servants who never speak,
dogs that bite like beasts.
There they see her black and thin
as a starving cat,
in the most vigorous and flourishing
of our beautiful Galician earth.
And these evils that afflict us
it's said she brings them all....
For, as happens in this life,
those to blame won't bear the burden![25]

---

[25] A poem that uses a folkloristic structure for political ends: to decry those who would evoke superstitions to explain poverty.

TO EVERYTHING ITS TIME

   From happy May, a fresh dawn
makes you smile in melancholy autumn,
and at Christmas, stiff limbed,
you happily warm yourself in August sun:
then you shivered fearful, and went
seeking deep and restless shade;
but lazy memory, too late
     reminded you
       that such sudden, strange
       and untimely changes
in struggles and worries, in this life,
were always the surest signs.
And in the heat lent to you in winter
     by some August sun
you felt only the mortal cold of fever
     that froze right to your bones.
     To everything its time
     And to each wild thing its den.[26]

---

[26] A poem that reminds us of Hamlet (Act 1, Scene 5) saying: 'The time is out of joint—O cursèd spite, / that ever I was born to set it right!'

*

　　　Beside the flowers, the girl
　　　sings happily her sweet song,
　　　and she's fair as a lily,
　　　pale as moonlight.
　　　Aside her sweet mouth, a pretty mole
placed by the Maker, shaped so perfectly
　　　　it charms us all.

　　　Tint of moonlight..., lovely colour!,
　　　two eyes like dark night,
　　　lips that speak smiling,
　　　and oh that mark... Beauty
greáter has been had by no creature,
than the beauty God willed you, lovely rose,
sweet, pure and gorgeous.

　Being loved, that's your hallmark,
loved more than anyone ever was,
and, what lucky fate!:
to be loved and to love well.
This is woman's very ambition
and the sole good she seeks unstinting
　　　in this wretched life.

　　　　But, beauty-marked girl,
　　　do you know the saying?
　　　Unlucky in love is
　　　she who bears such a mark.

	And they do say you're unlucky
despite the laughter on your lips
		that know no grievance.

	Sooner or later,
	in this thing of falling in love
	bad luck the traitor will
	fast be at work.
	And cast its spell on
innocent hearts and pure souls
		not meant for bitterness.

. . . .
. . . .
	Woe for the girl marked
	pale as moonlight!
	How she sings her song
	serene and unknowing
that she, marked by beauty, luck shall elude,
	that's how her life will go.

	Happy-go-lucky she sings
	some pretty chanson,
	that brings to her mind
	such cherished memories,
	that is thus like a prayer
that the sad soul lovingly murmurs
		asking God for fortune.

	And she doesn't realize, silly,
	and doesn't imagine, poor thing,
	that evil walks in love's footsteps,
	and her luck will wither
	if she's one born touched by beauty:

she of such exquisite marking
> will never know repose.

> Only grief awaits you,
lovely rose, marked by beauty;
greát grief following small,
one upon another will knock
at your door as they arrive;
and no one, such is destiny's power,
> can ever change your fate.

A ROLLING STONE

    She started out by thinking;
after that, she liked to think;
and from liking to desire,
goes more quickly as you sink.

    And daily wending downward,
downward without stop:
from desiring to the sinful,
you quicken as you drop.

WOE

   Why's it exist? Who is it? Where's its proud
home? Artful, how does it thrive?
Light sleep or passing cloud
is all it is for many, hardly leaves a trace.
Others feel its perfidious blows
lay siege to them with dark treachery
from start to end of life's slaving.
But they never see it, though they look
all round to avoid it; how many are there
who never feel its pestilent breath
in air or space, nor on earth nor on the sea,
though it's everywhere, ever damaging.

. . . .

   Evil is the child of hell, good that of heaven;
whose is woe? She-wolf
never sated, who redoubles her furor
on sighting a deep and bloody wound.
Where's it come from? What's it want? Why'd you let it,
mighty Maker, when you see us suffer?
Can't you tell, Lord, that its power suffocates
faith and love, in the spirit that'd faith in you?
How it hardens a heart that once
was every softness! How it kills
light in hope, so that hope's peaceful gleam
amid the stars is struck from existence,
light that lent new strength to tired feet
and renewed courage in the timorous soul!
All rots in its passage, its damned plaint
chokes everything forever:

it sticks its muck to everything.
And what a deep pit it digs around
whomever it pursues! How folk
flee from it so as to block the laments
its pain provokes, or the frightening
blasphemy that with trembling lip
it pronounces, biting!
No pestilence exists in life
that causes so much human horror
as it does to those touched by woe.

   And why not, if good turns its back,
if even sun does not shine where woe lives,
if the tap that gïves water daily
is poisoned, if even bread tastes
of dry nothing in the mouth, and endless sea
instantaneously goes dry
if woe wants to drown in its harsh waves;
as for the arms of death that weary it,
even death leaves woe alone!

   Take pity, Lord! Bar the shadow
that keeps casting eternal night
over the light of faith, love and hope!
Horrific shadow that obscures
shining stars in the heavens, that's made
new hell in this world, and a new world
where all courage loses its zeal
and all strength shatters without struggle,
where the long dark of pitilessness
bars every path that leads forward.

Kind Maker, with your potent breath,
dispel this horrible phantasm from us
and let woe come to an end;
enough already of aches, of wretched
weak flesh and of infallible death,
that torment and punish those sad ones who
having gone wrong, live banished
from the exalted home for which they sigh![27]

---

[27] Rosalía de Castro's reflections on *desgracia* merit note. The title in Galician translates, in one sense, to what it looks like: *disgrace*. Un-grace. Un-lightness, if grace is lightness as it is in the word 'graceful.' In fact, Rosalía de Castro speaks of what we today call depression. I titled 'Desgracia' in English as 'Woe' rather than depression, to widen the register of the title word a bit, yet to make a link with depressive illness, which often is exacerbated by the social. Rosalía's passionate social ire is evident in this poem, and it is no plaint, for even if depression touched her deeply (during the period she wrote these poems, there were political and familial and health setbacks), she was able to rise to speak, which many cannot. The struggle in Rosalía de Castro marks not simply melancholy but a steady rage. She touches and acknowledges a wrenched hole in the social and personal fabric and she does not draw back. Depression in her era had no pharmaceutical alleviation. Then, as today, women were more prone to it, or more prone to admit to it and admit to treating it. It's no coincidence that an early anti-depressant, Valium, was known as 'Mother's Little Helpers.' From market entry in 1963 to the end of patent in 1985, it was a top-selling drug in America. Along with it, drugs such as Quaaludes, marketed as a sleeping potion, found their way into our bloodstream as anxiety-repressants, and turned out to worsen depression and suicidal thoughts, further degrading the lives of women. In our time, the pharmacology of depression treatment is more sophisticated, but it still remains that depression, *desgracia*, is often an offshoot of societal precarity. The World Health Organization (WHO) has predicted that by 2020, major depressive illness will be second only to heart disease as the world's leading cause of disability. De Castro was ahead of her time. I don't think there's any poet in any language active in the nineteenth century who more clearly addressed depression as a women's and human health issue, as an issue provoked by migration and precarity.

*

    And so! When your most
ardent desire's fulfilled,
my constant laugh will then be
      just a laughter sad and dark.

    From my solitary corner
I'll look out for you serenely,
while on the heels of spring and summer
I'll see winter closing on you all.
      There's be no winter sadder,
      more harsh and wild...!

    As leaves drop from trees in autumn,
from your hearts will fall
the bright illusions you scatter over
      the cemetery earth
in which our dead sleep together
      in forgotten silence.

    Then in folds of dark shrouds
they'll appear before your very eyes,
sayyng: —I bet this wasn't what you sought
when you foolishly insulted heaven...
No doubt that wasn't it, unlucky ones,
      but... neither was it *this*...!
And in my corner I'll smile at myself
      with a sad and dark smile.

UNNESTLED

    Across mountains and fields,
paths and esplanades,
a single lonely dove flies on
alone from branch to branch.

    Her poor chicks trail behind her,
thirsty and so weak,
for she's found not a bit of food
to put into their beaks.

    She drags soiled plumage
that once was bright;
she drags, sullied and scratched now,
her weary broken wings.

    Oh poor dove, once so white
who was once so cherished!
Where did your glów go?
Your love, where did he wander?[28]

---

[28] Again, a migration song, seen through the condition of the woman and children left behind.

I CRAVE YOU, YOU CRAVE ANOTHER

—The pretty grand dame
of peerless beauty,
where's she off to at this odd hour,
in a night so dark?
Where's she so intent on going?

She's off through mud
in her silken slippers...
Through prickly görse the lady heads,
her husband left between fine sheets!
May God let him sleep soundly!

Let him sleep, and my eyes will watch
the most gorgeous lady
I've seen in the world and ever will;
gardener, I'll care for the rose
whose perfume's enjoyed by another.

I'll care for it, night and day,
without rest or peace,
for neither of those are for me.
Body and soul, I won't hold back;
I'll devote myself fully.

And even if she is not aware,
I know how much I care for her,
but such knowledge will be my end...
Fly, sweet dove; go, dear star,
someone valiant watches over you.

. . . .

Where's she going? The hidden
door creaks open slowly...
The murmur of stitched silks
swishes out upon the path
that goes from spring to mill...

   I can't see her, but she's there;
her sweet perfume reaches me,
I feel her footsteps,
and my heart, hurt
by pleasure, leaps a beat.

   Noble dame, pretty lady,
of all the hearts you cherish,
forgïve me, yes, forgïve me
if I follow you where you go:
don't you see you're in danger?

   In such a stormy night,
who planted such desire in you?
You'd even splatter mud on roses...!
And in my heart I discern
that you've no blessed host to save you.

   What if you meet the wandering souls?
What if the very ghost points its finger at you?
And fools you with its talk
and set the table to eat
amid thunder and lightning?

You'll not go alone, despite yourself,
you'll not go alone as long as I breathe,
for it'd be against God.
Lady, God does not allow
people to seek out danger.

Without you knowing that I follow,
I'll trail close behind you,
in case the devil tempts you.
And as long as it is not yet dawn
I will not leave you, my Lady.

—Farewell... farewell, lady of beauty;
to gïve in to such bad ways!
It wasn't wandering souls who spirited you off,
you were carried away by the devil.

My soul's gripped by shadows...
Oh, crazy love..., crazy love...!
That old saying says it well:
I crave you, you crave another.

*

—Be brave! For though you're pliable as wax,
    we are in danger here;
on the other side, freedom awaits you
    no one here will grant you.
—Let's go, my Lord, where you wish, let's go!

—So noble you are, my love, and striving;
but you tremble like a trapped doe;
now fortune's brought us together we can
both flee, my treasured love!
    —So let's flee, let's fleee!

    —Are you afraid, love o'my life,
to be found in my arms
and that, in sharing love, we'll die?
—Oh, no! It's pure happiness!
    But let's leave... leave...
and farewell, peace and virtue, my steadfast love!

SWEET SLEEP

    The angels flew down
to where she was,
made her a bed
of placid wings,
and bore her away
in the silent night.
    When at dawn of day
the bell tolled,
and in the steeple high
the lark sang out,
the angels themselves,
their wings folded,
—Why, they marmured,
why wake her up?...

*

  —Scared, I see the abyss
where I'm out walking now.
The heart is such a tyrant,
and it beats fierce for you, my love!
So I, unable to stop myself,
hear but one voice alone,
and where it wishes me to go,
unable to resist, I go...

  Today, at night, as all sleep,
through the window I will flee;
shadows will speed me onward...
Farewell, house of my birth!
  Honour I so did value,
sanctity of my home...
For love, I leave you all
and for all eternity!
  Maker...! You'll condemn me;
and I deserve it, yes I know;
but... go on, condemn me, Lord,
I'll suffer it by his side!

*

 —For life and for death
and forevermore
I asked you of God and God gave you me
for all eternity.
 —For life and for death
and forevermore,
I want to be yours and that you be
naturally Lord of me.
 —But she who wants this knows
she must have no dad, nor brothers,
nor man, if she's married,
nor children if she's mother.
 —What you say is shocking,
but I feel that it's true,
take me Lord for I'll go
wherever you want me to.
 —So come, for what's world matter
to whoever has eternity?
Together we must live,
together they must bury us,
and our bodies here,
and our souls there,
God wills that in eternal union
they'll be forevermore...

 As does the serpent to the bird,
and sparrowhawk to the dove,
he pulled her from her nest
and never there will she return.

AT THE TOMB OF ENGLISH GENERAL SIR JOHN MOORE FALLEN IN BATTLE AT ELVIÑA (CORUNNA) 16 JANUARY 1809

To my friend Maria Bertorini, native of Wales
A Coruña, 1871[29]

How far away, so far, from those dark mists,
green pines, and churning waves
that saw his birth! From his paternal home,
sky of the land that lovingly caressed him,
from the places, oh, of his longing, how far!...
It saw him fall under enemy blows
to never rise again, poor wretch!
To die as he did, upon foreign beaches,
die so young, abandon life
not yet done with life, still yearning!
To taste the fruit that could have been!
And instead of the wreath of laurels
that crowns the manly head of heroes,
to be lowered into the tomb silent and mute!

Oh white swans of the British Isles,
oh groves that border gallantly
along green banks of the bucolic rivers
and fresh fields where John once ran...!

---

[29] This poem, Byronic in tone, marks Rosalía de Castro's only venture into a form like the English ode. María Bertorini is the married name of María Margarita Jones, who had come from Cheshire to Iria Flavia (near de Castro's home in Padrón) with her husband Camilo Marcos Bertorini, Barcelona-born promoter of the first railway in Galicia. Angueira suggests that the dedication points to a shared Celtic link between peoples of the UK and those of Galicia. I think it simply points to a shared national respect for Moore among women who were neighbours. As *Corunna* was the usual British name for *A Coruña*, it seemed appropriate for the poem's English title.

If only his bitter sobbing sigh reaches you,
as with his last breath
he bids you farewell, with loving yearning,
sending to you the last thoughts
that from his mind easily escaped;
with what mourning, with what unspeakable grief
with what unequalled strangeness we would
bid farewell! to he who so far away, so very far,
from his country, alone, was lowered to eternity!

And the greát seat, the stilled drapery
of the forever-abandoned bed;
the cold ash of the hearth without flame,
the soft carpet that loyally maintains
a visibre mark of the Dead Man's foot,
the dog that awaits its absent master
and seeks him wandering down barren roads,
in the high grass of the overgrown lane
where once he did take solace in his walks,
the ever constant murmur of the fountain,
where he would go sit in fading afternoon...
How they will speak endlessly of Moore
in his own clipped and stiff language,
the eyes, oh, of those who wept for him!
And nevermore....., nevermore, oh sadness,
will he return to where they await him!
He went bravely, to do battle in glory.
He went! He went!... and did not return, for death
scythed him down there in foreign fields,
like the flower that falls where its own seed
will find no soil in which to root.

So you fell, poor John, far from the tomb
where you'd thought you'd rest with your own.

In foreign soil your bones still sleep
and those who loved you and still remember,
in gazing at the waves of the veiled Ocean,
say grieving, from your native beaches:
—He's out there, across that wild sea;
there he remains, perhaps, perhaps forever,
in a tomb where no one will weep, or cherish
the beloved ashes of the one we've lost...!
And sad winds and quiet breezes
so beloved by those dead who sleep far
from their native soil, come to refresh you
in summer's hot nights, and carry
you laments in a caress of wings,
soft sighs, loving echoes;
a teardrop still wet, that dampens
the dry stone of the cold mausoleum,
bringing wild perfumes from your country.

But what a beautiful and unequalled abode
your mortal remains had the luck to find!...
God did not wish for you,
noble stranger, an alien home!...
There's no poet or dreaming spirit
who, on contemplating in autumn
the seä of dry yellowed leaves
that cöver your mausoleum with love,
who, on contemplating at fresh dawn
the smiling light of the month of May
that always comes in joy to visit you,
won't say: —Thus too when I die, that I might
lie in peace in this flowering garden,
close to the sea... far from graveyards!...
May you never hear, oh Moore,
bitter tears, nor whining prayers,

nor may other dead call to ask you in deepest night
to share in the awkward sway of ghostly dances.
Only the gentle breath of the bud that opens,
of the flower that withers its last farewell,
crazy foments, childish laughter
of pretty children who come to hide
behind your white stone, unfrightened.
And, at times, and often, I hope! you'll hear the sighs
of ardent love, that wind lifts up
God only knows where... may they
keep you peerless company in your final home.
And the sea, the sea, wild sea that röars
a roar that rocks you in your cradle,
lives at your side, comes to kíss the stones
of the loving ground that holds you in its love,
and around your resting place lets roses grow!...
Rest in peace, rest in peace, oh Moore!

   And you who love him, people of Albion,
watchful of your honour, rest easy.
Galician earth is noble earth—the Maker's
granted it much beauty—; it knows how
to honour all who merit honour,
and honoured yes, as he merited, was Moore.
He is not lonely in his tomb; a people
watch with compassionate respect over
this foreigner whom traitorous death
kept far from his own, and whom of strangers
had to ask his final haven.

When you cross the sea's waves
to come to visit your brother,
lend to his tomb your ear's caress,
and if you feel the ashes moving,
and if you hear indefinable voices,
and if you hear what those voices say,
your soul will feel consoled.
He'll tell you that nowhere in the world
could he have found a better tomb
outside of England than this loving refuge!

*

I

   With what grace you sway
your body lithe
out on the dance floor
with that gallant beau,
just as the gentle alder
branches sway in north wind;
and leaves one upon another
yellow-tinged
keep falling, tangling
in your curly locks,
crowning you with sadness,
as withered, oh God in heaven,
as the sadness your own thoughts
settle in your soul...
It's that autumn's fleeting!
Winter's on its way!

   But in the depths
of the pleasant valley, gentle
winds still serenely blow,
bringing perfumes from heaven.
Even now on lush banks
flecked with cling-peach blossoms
where the Miño River flows
majéstic and somnolent,
the sweet final sigh

of summer can be heard,
which lingers sleeping still
in rosemary and lavender,
just like a ray of hope
lingers in your heart.

II

But if there's one bad sign,
and bad sign it is indeed,
it's that the speeding currents
never turn back.
What is it you hope for, when hope
pays you no mind?

Onward, woman,
bring your pilgrimàge to an end;
though you may not want to stop,
out there fierce hurricanes
and waves will snatch you away
from your unlucky fate.

You've still got faith! You'll
have it, poor dear, in your ills;
you'll have it in the thorns
that come to torment you:
in the poisonous bile that
you'll drink without thirst;
in the hard and bitter bread
that will feed you.

    Gentle waves never
turn back in the sea;
your stubborn destiny will never
be soothed by good luck,
nor will happiness revive you
with its sweet rest;
for only the sleep of death
lets sad ones rest in peace.

    So bring to a close
your sad pilgrimage,
for all born under a bad sign,
are dogged by bad signs.
On wings of woe
your destiny flies,
and speeding currents
never turn back.

WITHOUT EARTH

—Shush, oh winds of night;
shush, fountain of Serena,
for at the end of Trompas alley
    I want to hear who arrives!

All the winds died down,
the fountain spilled more quietly,
and I saw that they came to bury
    her very heart.

Later I saw her still alive
in fields and in the meadows:
she'd gone looking for a tomb
    to give it earth.

She found none, and this is why
though her heart's dead
its gangrene, visible to us,
    glows yet.

*

> *Some see black,*
> *others white,*
> *yet all of them*
> *are out of sync.*

I

 —Be astute if you know how to;
avenge insults if you can;
 to one who dishes them at you, repay him;
but to one who never insults, do the same;
 for the morals of saints
don't always match the morals of men.

  This a Galician mountain man and rough,
fed up with rancour and humiliation,
on his deathbed advised his son,
inheritor of his troubles and his name.

II

 —Be innocent and always loyal,
  pardon whoever offends you,
do well each day by friend and foe,
and with door unlocked, attend without fear;
there's but one God and one morality that saves
  Eve's sad offspring.

This the poor widow
of the mountain man, dying in poverty,
resignedly said to her son...
and to her Maker she gave up the ghost, serene.

III

And he presided over her
all alone in his sighs and tears;
no priest in those parts would give
a charity burial to the poor.
   In a corner of the yard,
where prickly nettles grew,
without cross, sign or gravestone,
she lay lost and laid to rest,
and her son sad and lonely,
turned back angry to his empty home.

   —My Dad advised me one way, he thought,
and my Mom another;
and though she was saintly and of good conscience,
he had experience and knowledge in spades.
   I am son of both...
so I'll cleave my legacy in two:
My mother: do well to those who do you well,
My father: your very bones demand revenge.

SAD RECOLLECTIONS

    One afternoon out in Castile,
the sun beat down as it had always done,
beaming in that desert.

    Clear, burning, and insolent,
excuse me, but it's no way to act,
charring folks like that,

    and joyfully shrivelling
the poor simple plant,
the fountain, the parched rivers.

    One afternoon, oh what sadness,
the sun attacked me so perfidiously,
seeing me so hopeful!

    Where's it going to stop?
I thought, gazing at sky
so as to turn my eyes from earth.

    Because the sky was, oh yes,
more or less as blue
as ours in Galicia.

    But the earth, good Grief!
Lord, is it possible
that you made it?

But why do I find it strange
since in all of your acts
you never act badly?

You created those sad plains,
but you did it, clement Maker,
just for Castilians.

Ay! Every dove has its nest,
every rabbit its burrow,
every soul its soulmate.

That's what I intoned
that afternoon, memory
of dark melancholy.

And meanwhile, I gazed
across the flat expanse of plain,
at earth that was blanching;

at the greát weary pinewood,
its dark stain without end;
at the village, scorched in colour.

And between soil and firmament,
the wind was stirring
clouds of thick dust.

Desert's true image,
with desert's burning breath,
desert's hot courage!

In the distance, the muletrain passed,
the herd of bulls drew closer,
the unwell sheep bawled.

And on the scorched bramble,
fleeing the ardent sun,
a small bird rested.

Oh my, its tiny anxiety!
Sadness weighed me down,
as if I were buried alive.

Memories of beautiful land,
calm with freshness,
ached in my weeping soul.

For that parched river
shrouded in fetid fogs,
provokes fevers, provokes chills.

Suddenly I heard a song,
a song that moved me
till it took my breath away.

It was a Galician melody,
it was the *alalá*... that made
my heart jump.

With a strange rhythm,
sweet, as if in love;
savage, as if in agony!

    Caked in sweat and dust,
scythes on shoulders,
through those desert fields

    a team of harvesters came...
And it was they, they,
the charmed bearers of song!

    Farewell, scorched pines!
Farewell, sun-grilled soils
and desolate headlands!

    I closed my eyes and saw...:
saw freshets, meadows and plains
spread at my feet.

    When I opened them again,
dying of yearning,
I wallowed in my tears.

    And could not stop my crying
until the moment I was borne
away from Castile.

    They took me from that place
so as not to entomb me there.

*

   Frigid months of winter
that I love with all my heart,
months of brimming rivers
and sweet love of the hearth.
   Months of storms,
image of the pain
that afflicts the young
and cuts them down in flower.
   It's come, and throughout autumn
that causes leaves to fall,
lay me to sleep in leaves
and I'll dream myself away.
   And when the pretty sun
of April smiles again,
may it light my repose,
and no more my suffering.

*

I

   It was in the month of May,
in the month of love, of plants and flowers,
month of suave prefumes
and transparent colours.
Of morning trills of little birds,
of fresh and candid dawns,
of fleeting clouds,
of afternoons asmile and golden.
When the sea is blue, the sky serene
like a sleeping baby,
rivers gentle, high the stars,
more faded is the moon,
yet also more beautiful,
with a peerless grace all of its own.
It was, in short, a time when all in this life
smiled on mortals with the happy, splendid
virginal smile of spring
that invites all to love and be lucky.

   Invites all...oh! If only fate
could máke it so;
for there's one who, cloaked in the dark
of his own sadness,
sees only, in lovely spring,
in warming sun and in the rose
glistening with fresh dew of morning,
a sad bad omen that awakens
thoughts of mourning and misfortune.

II

It was a morning in the month of May
on which the angels seemed to sing,
while breezes gently moaned
in a loving lament;
on which the rivulet trickling past the curtain
lightly murmured who knows what,
and the flight of restless swallows
who twittered in the air,
at the sight of wise clouds
foretold adventures and pleasures.
Morning of enchantments,
just what the spirit craves
as it waits and trusts;
morning that calls every being
to pleasure and joy,
apart from the sad soul
that in his very being knows not
what it is to feel relief and calm,
where sweet pleasure starts,
where the cruelty of pain ends.

III

Oh kind guardian angel, you
who slowly bat white wings
around the afflicted spirit,
to touch it with blessed consolations
you bear us from the infinite,
where oh where have you been,
and why in such dark sorrow

did you leave that one sad soul?
Faith, hope, charity,
source of eternal beatitudes,
from luckier regions, you
come to calm our bitterness...
where are you, doing what?
When the one who places trust in you,
struggling alone with worry and agony,
orphaned, calls you without response?

IV

   Among all those he insistently hated,
among all who he loved spitefully,
a sad one condemned to hard fate
plunged his gaze into the wild Cantabrian surf
wondering if
in such a deep tomb
the huge space of another world might be visibre.
And with adamant spirit,
so as to touch the clear liquid
he raced in a dizzying run
as if in the lure of the mysterious abyss
a strange power leads him to death.

   And he said: —Farewell, life!! Farewell, torment,
that with slow martyrdom
robs even my dreams of hope!
As for my misfortune,
I'll breák the grip of its strong arm
to go where there is no pain, or change,
where worry is buried in repose.

And you, evil passion loosed in me
you were my God and my punishment,
if you still want to kill me, die with me!

   The sad one stopped, and fearsome
huge waves with manes of foam
twisted back upon the sands,
inciting the poor wretch
to end the battle
that had started in his breast.

   But a soft sound
suddenly found the perturbed ear
of that unlucky chump...
And he listened astounded to
an invisible being whose alluring talk
in soft and celestial melody
suavely and gently told him:

   —Stop right there at your life's
shore, cowardly sentinel;
don't think that by fleeing the present
you'll pull the veil from eternity!
Try to take the path of life
between the roses and the bile;
don't leap into your tomb
before the Maker asks it of you.
No offspring of Eve is ever freed
finally from their pain
until death comes of its own accord.
After having crossed
the huge deserts of the infinite,
you'd return to the world in spirit
to suffer, and pay for your crime.

By day and night,
without rest or release
you'd find yourself stuck to that breast
where the ungrateful heart beats
not for you but for the sake of repetition.
And in that thought
with implacable clarity you'd read
treacherous betrayal, bitter oblivion
unhidden by veils or tricks.

   —Oh God, all-powerful Maker!
What horrific torment!

   —No one can reverse the power of destiny
miserable or benign;
nor is it easy for anyone
to alter their fate.
Only those who wait and hope will triumph...
So get back to life and wait resigned.

   And he turned to live, having repented
though sad and hurt
was that poor wretch:
he asked God's pardon for his sin,
and G-d, compassionate,
gave him holy peace and sweet oblivion.

WHAT'S UP?

    Always a plaintive *oh!,* a qualm,
a desire, an anguish, an ache...
At times it's a star that dazzles,
at others it's a ray of sun;
it's the leaves that fall from trees,
then it's flowers that burst in fields,
      and it's the wind that moans;
      and it's the cold, and heat...
And it's neither wind nor sun, nor is it the cold;
      it's not..., no it's just
the soul assailed, poetic and sensitive,
      all lashed by disappointment
      railing at everything.

*

—You, charming and white as snow,
    and prettiest of all among the best;
you, around whom men flit buzzing
as bees do toward a rose
(folk who, and it's the same for women,
are capable of every betrayal);
you never love, but are loveable;
you never gïve forth, they gïve forth to you;
if they wound you, my beloved, laugh;
if they cheat you, my love, don't cry.
The age of Corinne[30] is obviously long gone,
    and just as you suffer now
        when it's not the time to speak,
    you'll just rage later, when you can.
—Rage? you say. I think you're lying!
    —Yes, yes, rage loudly;
for the itch and needle of rage
is the tasty sauce of passion.
What would happen to poor stomachs, oh gawd!,
without absinthe?
    And as for the heart in our day,
where'd it be without rage, my love?

---

[30] A reference to Madame de Staël's *Corinne, Or Italy* (1807).

RUINS
(Late Day Serenade)

Rosalía de Castro's translation of Ventura Ruiz de Aguilera from Spanish, translated from Galician by EM, without rhyme. A mirror of a mirror, a mise en abyme...

    November heaved a sigh
as tired and alone I took a seat
beneath the crumbling wall,
ancient rampart and village border.
    Through a house of cracks
left agape by time to lizards,
today the salamander watches
gazing coldly at the ravages around it.
    Nasty and pale,
creeping nettle and sickly sour radish,
the many fronds moán
when the wind moves them.
    Capstones crown
the destroyed portal of the chapel,
that stands in the churchyard,
skeleton in the dust of altars.
    Already at the sacred hearth
no mother kindles fire while praying,
and from soot-black stones
wind has long swept the ashes;
    and from the ancient arches
and columns, stones jar loose and fall
just as teardrops do
from inconsolably sad eyes.

How the rotting leaves
fall from the branch where they were born,
rubble left from life that
once charmed these quiet woods.

　　And the river seems
almost dried up its pebbled bed,
miserable relic of a channel
once clean, copious, serene!

　　How the hills are aflame
in autumn sun as light wanes,
while shadowy the night
quietly surprises the valley.

　　The tolling in the distance
of a bell sighing prayers:
the dying afternoon
says its fond farewell to religion.

　　And the little owl hovering
also cries its chill predictions,
like one dead without tomb,
who wanders a graveyard's edge.

　　As its wings beat,
its voice awakens sleepy echoes,
and seems to resound
behind what passes pensive and austere:

　　the mysterious roár
of visions marshalled by fears,
pale skeletons screaping long shrouds
darkly across the ground.

　　Oh may the populace waken
from its eternal repose,
exhausted pilgrims
finding new energy in rest.

　　They take up their trek again
at the sweet dawn of serene day,

its splendid light dressed
modestly in a veil of cloud.
   But the spell ends,
a moment later; thus the remains
of mortal illusions fill
the breast with soulful feeling.
   And once again from the wall
stones crumble and gïve way,
and the leaves to this cadence
keep falling from yellow trees,
      just as teardrops
fall from sad and inconsolable eyes
to the rubble left from life that
once charmed these quiet woods.
   All things pass; shadow
always follows on the light of clear sky
and old age expires.
Youth is, oh, but fleeting memöry.
   You alone do not perish,
oh, spirit that sighs in its cell!
But death's compassionate hand
will finally break your chains.
   The fragile vase of your immortal essence
now in pieces will remain,
and rising into air, it
will go seek out eternal love.
   To the land you'd lost,
you'll fly up gently from the soil
that your wings brushed
when you fell into desert from the world.
   There, ay! you recall it sadly,
just as a banished wretch recalls
her homeland and its blue skies
from the banks of foreign rivers.

*

    Squeal of carts from Ponte,
sad bells from Herbón;
when I hear you, my heart-
strings shatter.

    Onion sellers who come and go
along the road through Adina,
when you pass the burial ground
go gently and slowly.

    I know it's said the dead don't hear,
but when I go speak to my own,
I'm certain that, though silent,
they hear my grief intoned.

MANDOLIN SONG

   With the deadly sword
sunk into my chest,
my spirit in shadow
and body in muck
darker than death,
than the lowest of earth,
gobs of blood
I was weeping.

   Suddenly in the thick
of brown fog
with rare harmony
arose a song...
How fresh and sweet,
how light and strange
it resounded in the hidden
caverns of the beach!

   My aches were calmed
as thirst is with water,
as the poor parched person
at the fountain finds peace.
Trapped in my eyes
the tears remained,
while immobile and
suspenseful, I listened.

   From times remote,
from distant ages,
from serene nights

forever ended,
that singing brought me
so many memories,
not dead... sleeping,
who knows in what tombs!

   I thought I'd heard it
in the fields of Italia,
being perhaps queen,
perhaps but a slave,
on the shore of the Bosphorus,
at the castle window ...
But deep love always
I felt in my soul.

   What strange dreams
had awakened in me,
from the unknown music
of the mellifluous song?
Of former lives,
that in recollection
calmed the aches
of present cares?

   Who can say?
Mysteries of fragile
human nature,
no one can explain;
I only know that, feeling
consolation in my soul,
I loved from that moment
the mandolin's song.

*

>   Pallid virgins with candid faces,
> Hallowed gents with unfurrowed brows,
>>   noble matrons,
>>   austere nuns,
> and even those who seem never
>>   to have touched their soles
>>   to the muck of earth,
> in their consciences, hidden, who knows
>>   how defiled they are?

>>   But sure as there's wide rivers,
>>   and immense seas,
>>   and lakes unprobed
> and torrents that uproot griefs,
> in all spheres of this world
>>   there's no water washes
>>   a defiled conscience clean;
>>   and those that defile themselves
>>   defiled they remain.
> They'll only wash clean with the copious tears
>>   of repentance!

VANITY

A few rich folk try to sink the poor,
and as for the poor, it's the greát they sink,
    all to puff themselves up,
    and act proud till they die.
Vanity, how you waltz amid men,
right till the gates of death open!
    But when they're lowered into the hole,
    all of them are equals;
    dust turns to dust
    and with it, pride.

*

Hurry, Álvaro of Anido,
live a lot in a little time,
goad your horse
and in goading it, rupture it.
What's one noble horse?
What're two or three hundred?
What counts, Álvaro Anido,
    is arriving early.

Run from one end to another,
map all the dark caves,
climb up on the locomotive,
rise up in aerial balloons,
and scuttle like a crab
over the wide space of the void:
you're a man, Álvaro, you'll give out,
    running and running.[31]

---

[31] Iria Flavia, near Padrón where Rosalía de Castro lived, was the home of the Bertorinis and their son-in-law John Trulock, two of the families from the UK who helped bring the first railway to Galicia, inaugurated in 1873. Locomotives would have been a potent symbol of progress heard nearby, as de Castro finished this book. Even so, she seems sceptical of travelling by speeding over the surface and past everything...

*

   —You claim that marriage
is blessed and good. So be it,
but Saint Anthony[32] never wed,
even though the very devil
tried to get him to try.

   As many hairshirts as possible, yes,
and heaps of penance;
but I notice that no saint wished
to shoulder the heavy cross
of the married.

   Not even the holy fathers,
of whose scriptures we have plenty,
along with all their hallelujahs,
wanted to sink their holy feet
into that kind of muck.

   From every angle,
matrimony, you're a noose;
you're a temptation to hell,
but I'll get married..., for winter's coming...
I need someone to warm my feet!

---

[32] Saint Anthony of Padua is saint of marriages and of reconciliation of couples. His feast day is in June, considered the month of marriages. An anti-clerical poem for it makes light of the holiness of wedlock, finding only one good reason for getting married: warmth for cold feet!

*

    Now hair of black,
much later hair of grey;
now pearly whites,
tomorrow yellowed incisors;
today cheeks all rosy,
tomorrow wrinkled leather.
    Black death, dark death,
cure for aches and folly,
why don't you just slay us gals
before the years do?

*

—May you end up, by God,
writhing like a snake in sand;
may the water you go to drink
clog your mouth with weeds.
May you beg and never find
rest, peace, or protection;
and even dead with hunger,
may you end up against a wall.
   —Curse, mouth, curse
while I'm heading down the road:
the curses of fallen women
never work on soldiers.

*

I've a sickness that's incurable,
a sickness since I was born,
and this inimical sickness
will send me to the grave.

Healers, surgeóns,
medical doctors.
for this infirmity of mine,
there's no remedy among humans.

So stop turning pages
with diligence or with none;
in the books of your sciençe,
for me there's nothing in them.

You have your doubts? There's none
in what I'm saying, doctors;
even if you hate to hear it, there's bitterness
no syrup sweetens.

You're angry because you think
I overstate my case?
Well have a go then..., all hands to work:
try and cure me, friends.

My sickness and my suffering
are nothing but my heart.
Dig it out of me without flinching!
Then... make me live!

*

   Pleasure, for scabies, relieves the itch;
without it, the itch takes over;
and to ring true, affliction
has to hurt deeply.
There's no suffrance in bleeding tears
at the feet of your beloved.
To live far from him, and forgotten,
this, yes, is truly rótten!

*

   —It's true any person can
be bad or good;
but to come from solid stock
is better, if you would.
   Your ma and pa were gypsies,
today you're a marquis,
even so, when all's said and done,
back to where we came, we flee.
   Dog born of a fox,
that they claim is loyal:
if it's not killing chickens
it's that it's been foiled.

   So sang a blind bard
at the Assumption fair,
making listeners laugh
as it was pretty rare.
   And they glanced at each other
as if wishing to say:
—Scratch your own ïtch, brother;
I don't itch in any way.

*

You write some verses and... what verses!
Never seen anything like them:
each line armed with pebbles,
knuckledusters every one,
as if they're made for thwacking
those who read them in the nose.

*

    A child trembles in the damp portal...
Hunger and cold
mark his angélic face
still pretty, but worn and dull.

    Ragged and shoeless, on the stones
his poor wee feet were
split by the ice of winter.
He rests them tentatively;
they look like they've been cut by blades
of razor wire.

    Like dog without hayrick or master,
whom all despise,
he hides trembling in a corner
under the stairs.
As a lily droops when it withers,
the golden-haired innocent
also droops, faint with hunger,
and rests his face on the stones.

    And as he sleeps,
sad image of pain and poverty,
they file past, *to adore the Most High.*
What Pharisees, these exalted of the earth:
even seeing the orphanhood of the innocent
does not calm
the greedy thirst of the rich.
Anguish oppresses my heart.

Maker! God of Heaven!
Why are their souls so dark and hard?
Why are there orphans on earth, bountiful Maker?

   But it's not in vain that the book of
mysteries stays sealed...
Glory, power and happiness pass...
All on this earth passes. We hope!

IV

HOMELAND

HUSH!

On green riverbanks, on shimmering beaches
and in the rough cliffs of our towering sea,
there are eerie folksongs, of spells unknown,
that only with us share their playful plea.

In the loving shade of our oakwoods,
and in our fresh meadows of vivid splendoúr,
and in the murmur of springs, there are cherished spirits,
that offer loving words to those born here.

And in our mountains and in these our skies,
as long as there's life here, as long as being exists,
there are bright suave colours, of humid transparency,
of uncertain vagary, that to us alone gïve bliss.

You who were born on different shores,
who are warmed by the flame of a living glare,
and who need this burning sun to live,
hush, if the charms of our home you don't share,
just as we, not seeing those of yours, go quiet.

HOMELAND

*

*My sweet abode, my hearth,
you're worth more to me
than your weight in gold.*

    From Santiago to Padrón,
I came in driving rain,
bare-legged and shoeless,
without dinner or breákfast.
On the road I spotted
rich things to buy,
and although I wanted them
I had no way to pay.
From restaurants rose aromas
of tasty things,
but those who lack money
have to walk on by.
I arrived at my house
exhausted from walking,
I didn't have a crumb there
on which to sup.
My sight was fading,
it was hard to hang on.
I went to a neighbour's house
that was full to the rafters;
I begged a little cornbread
and he wouldn't lend.
Tears fell from me
I was so ashamed.
I returned to my wee house
lit up by the moon;

I lookd in every crevice
to see what I could find:
I found some flour dust,
a small fistful was all,
at the bottom of the bread-bin
and gave praise to Gdd.
I wanted to light the fire,
but had no wood to burn.
I went to ask an old woman;
all she would share
was a stick of green bramble
to drive me raving mad.
I was sad as night
from crying just to cry;
I nabbed a fist of straw,
from my mattress it came;
I searched the whole stable
praying the whole while,
and saw a few bits of kindling
and ferns, thanks to God.
My miraculous Saint Anthony,
the home fire's alight!
I put the pot on the flame
with water to heat,
while I scratched
in the ashes, I saw the glint:
a lucky penny!
Oh Virgin of Pilar!
Out I dashed
and bought some salt,
happier than at Christmas
I returned to my yard,
and in my garden plot
I spied some cabbage leaves.

With a little old lard
that I'd wisely saved,
and with the fine flour,
I had enough to dine.
I made a glorious brotth
as tasty as the sea;
made a few dumplings
that were something to envy;
after I had eaten up
I said another prayer;
and after having prayed
I hung up my wet clothes,
for not a single thread was dry
I'd been soaked so bad.
And while I was drying myself,
I broke out in song
> so that they'd hear me
> everywhere:

My hearth, my home,
to me you're worth more
than your weight in gold.

PRIDEFUL

   Colour of lead, the clouds pile up;
the waves of the sea turn slow;
and roaring with a frightful sound
     the hurricane shows.

   How heavy is the sky and sad;
how dark, how black it's turning!
We'll light the vigil candle,
     against the storm.

   Riding on the wings of angels,
sent by the Almighty they'll race
the lightning bolts that frighten evil
     with their flashing.

   We'll burn nine leaves of olive,
to keep all evil away,
and to free us from the bolts of light
     that kill us.

   The Trisagion prayer we all chorus,
bow down and adore our God;
for if it thunders, it's that he wants to remind us
     he's greát and immortal.

   Holy, holy! They say to each other
     children and mother;
All, no, for one, prideful and irascible,
     won't pray.

But the heavens drown in thunder
and blind lightning's glow.
Oh what a night! What terrible night
    of storms!

The Lord's irate... Bow down!
Oh, wicked of the earth, tremble!
Whoever survives this night alive
    will tell the tale.

—Mother, the tawny cow
shakes in her stall beside you.
Do you think that she sinned?
Will a bolt of lightning kill her?

—It's not her who sinned,
you lousy Christian, it's you,
you've been an unrepentant sinner
from the minute you were born.

—And the poor tawny cow
pays, I asked, for my sinning?
—You pay; when she's dead,
tell me, whatever will you eat?

POOR WOMAN SO DEAF...!

—There atop the mountain,
smoke rises from the chimneys...
Courage, old creaky body!
Carry me there, legs.
Slowly, ever so slowly,
stop here, sit there,
you'll get there, Joanna,
up where home fires are lit.
Hail Creátor, holy Virgin!,
today, maybe... maybe... perhaps...
you'll have seven mugs
of good broth, to eat for supper,
and a bread chunk with pork
or salt-pressed sardines,
for the mountaineers are men
who gïve freely, when they gïve.
After that, you'll warm at a blaze
huge as a bonfire,
and when you're warmed well,
to sleep... right till morning!

And the old woman climbed up
the steeps of the *Mar de Ovellas*
one eye on the ground,
the other on the smoking chimneys.

All the while, afternoon sun
was setting in the pines,
and it lights the shady forests
with sad rays.

From *Anxos* the pretty valley
shows off its green mantle
there in the peaceful dell
where soft breezes swirl.
Here spring, there creek,
water glittering in the grasses,
golden, as the last
ray of sun rests there.
Quiet, gentle calm
reigns high and low;
night comes quietly,
gently, starless.
Not a single light
glows in the firmament, for thick
fog rides out
across ethereal plains.
It starts to drizzle, dark
all around, even the familiar
is hardly recognizable,
neither road nor path.
But regardless,
the brave are truly brave,
and the old woman climbs up, up
the steeps of the *Mar de Ovellas,*
one eye on the ground,
the other on the houses smoking,
for a light glow-ed there,
and she heads to it
murmuring: —Upward, Joanna:
there's a feast ahead or I'm a fool.

   Experience teaches all,
and she had long experience;

that's why she wasn't wrong to think
that up there a feast awaited.

   Oak burned in the fire,
and around the hearth sat
girls with joyful eyes,
grandmas with long white locks,
old gals who roll sleeves
and clack the castanets,
the godchildren of the house
from all over the village,
and friends and inlaws,
cousins and other relations
all together, and even the priest
and the veterinary surgeon.
A blind man with hurdy-gurdy
alongside a blind woman
who sure can play tambourine
and make castanets chatter;
an armless man, a gïmp, a madwoman
and other poor folk, all squished
on a bench for ten aside the hearth,
so jammed in none more could fit
though a few more wanted to.
All arriving, arriving,
all sniffing out a party,
and no one was sent away
by the rich mountaineer's wife;
for there's plenty for all, today
they were cooking fresh meat,
heaps of it, and making
cauldrons of congee.
A sheep was butchered, big
as a bull, and a calf

large as a cow, and plump
as a little sow.
The wine flows, cinnamon-
hued wine of the Ribeiro;
and for the riffräff
there's also local slosh,
on the tart side but fresh
and scrumptious as strawberries.
An ovenful of white cornbread
bakes, gold-topped, mixed with rye
and a little bit of butter.
This *broa* is as rich as cake,
you can't get enough of it;
it's even more savoury
than the specially chosen loaves
lugged in triple baskets from Santiago
by the bakerwomen.
In short, there was food all over,
and the wine gladdened
folks so much that dark sadness
went wild with envy.
The poor folks who'd come there
to find warmth and table,
told yarns that made all laugh,
all the girls and grandmas,
some in verse, some in prose,
and they spoke in every language,
goading each other
to create even better couplets.
But the hurdy-gurdy player wins
with help from his companion,
both boosted by the white wine
that wet their throats.

—Hail to our blind bards!
folk shouted from time to time
and the bard yelled louder:
—Bravo gents! Bravo ladies!,
especially the prettiest one
who just gave me a hug.
Woo-woo-woot! And he whoops
until the very stones were deafened,
and the blind woman shook the tambourine,
the blind man touched the keys,
and to the beat of *zong, zong*
the girls danced up a storm.
And the poor folk said, adding
fuel to the fire: —What a party!
No need to wander outside today
on an empty stomach!
And they grin and stare
at the bales of fresh straw,
where they'll sleep all warm
like cracklings in broth,
while the wind wails outside
and dogs howl out on the range.

    Now almost midnight,
it's time to start wrestling,
the boys with the girls,
marshalling their forces
and basking in compliments,
end up on the floor.
If you could see how strong
the girls are in the fray!
They gïve the boys a start
with their tiny gripped hands!

—One's down aleredy... it's a man...
She won, she won!
Yay for the pretty girl!
Yay for girl mountaineers!
Yay for them, they sure can wrestle!
—She cheated! he answers
in shame. —I was trapped, coz if not,
a hundred like her couldn't beat me.
—What kind of trap was it... for bats...?
I beat you...
     —No.
          —Yes.
               —You beat me!

And in the fervour was heard:
Tap! tap! tap!, the sound of a stone
on the door.
          —Who's that? they asked.
—I'm a poor old woman
who's lost on this mountain...,
she responded, her voice in a tremour.
Won't you shelter me a bit,
for it's raining and thundering?
—May God keep you; it's aleredy late,
there's no room, they answered.
—What'd you say, ma'am? I'm deaf
as a capstone... my dear.
Open the door, and may the On High
bless you...
          —Poor old woman...
a little further on, not far at all,
there's more doors; go knock there.
—What'd you say, dear lady? Look
it's a wild night out here

and I'm scared the wolves
will eat me...
                —God almighty! As if!
There's no wolves here, go on, go on,
God keep you, there's another village
close.
—What'd you say, ma'am?
—Off you go, don't be stubborn,
there's no room here
for rich or poor, yeáh!
—Whazzat, my dear? I'm deaf,
I can't hear even earsplitting noise.
Brrrrrr, it's cold, my lady!
You who are so charitable,
let me in, and I'll go rest
in the stable with the animals.
Brrrr.... I'm dying of cold!
argh! aughoaua! argh! aughoaua!
What a cough..., God help me..., brrr!
I can't take it!
                —Okay, come in,
and if you've nowhere to sit
the horse trough will have to do;
said the lady, who had
a heart of butter.
—God bless you, sweet lady!
You'll find reward
in heaven... open, my jewel,
the old woman quickly exclaimed.
—What, she's not deaf, she heard!
they said from inside, while
pulling the bolt back
from the door.

                    —Whazt? my dear?
I didn't hear a thing, I'm
just sensitive, that's all...
                    —Oh I'll just bet
you're not lying! Come, come,
get inside...
                    —Blessed and good
night to you, my dear sirs...
Jeez, they're still partying,
it's jammed in here!
They'll still be here in a year, I wager.
God bless them all... the Lord
gave them fistfuls of luck
and there you go...
                    —Amen, amen!
Find a spot at the fire
and warm yourself up...
                    —Whatz you say?
I'm deaf as a stone,
and haven't had a crumb
since last night, and in my veins
my blood's stock-still
with cold...
                    And while
she said this, she drew close
to the fire so companionable
with the other wretches, and squeezed
in their midst, men and women all.
She jumped over the blind man,
and say what you like,
still shaking with cold
and deaf as a stone,
to hear her say it, she grabbed
the best spot, with greát humility,

and the fire flared warm where
she sat.
    —Ay, old woman!
you're not the only one
here! —What a pushy
broad! another wretch told her
with a face to rob milk
from babies.
    —Whazt, my boy?
(smiling she replied,
settling in more cozily)
as for me, like it or not
I look after my own; in heaven
the Maker can take care of me...
    —Bosh! it seems
you're trying to mock us folk...
—Phht, what's with that decrepit Judas!
She even looks like a poker.
—If I'd like a pint, my dear?
If they'd gïve me one, I'd just
sip at it once in awhile,
for I'm parched with thirst,
and hunger, and cold...
    —Howl on,
dog! Never saw a deaf woman
so skinny and sneaky.
Is she kit of some fox?
—Is she grabbing at a bone? They
just wanted to kid her. My Gawd!
But hunger was stárk in her;
—Just bring me what's left
sitting charred in the fire,
and I'll set to gnawing it
with the one fang I've got left.

    All laughed at her answer
and... —Though God wouldn't back me,
said the blind bard, that deaf woman
knows more than I do, I say!
—She deserves bread and sop
and I'll gïve it her, old dear,
because wherever it comes from
I always love wisdom.
Eat your fill! Here's a chunk
and some wine; drink,
drink on my tab
to the heálth of mountain lasses,
said the hostess, and passed a plate
heaped high with tripe
to the wretch; and wine, and as much
white bread as she wanted; she stuffed
herself until her belly was tight
as a tambourine. She's nearly
bursting... but she battled
back, and didn't even
crack, and by the next day
she was waddling bent over.

   —Take it easy, said the hostess
when she left. Just saying
don't come back here
as long as you're deaf.
—What'za say, my dearest?
the old woman responded laughing.
I'm deaf as a brick;
even if you split my head open, I can't hear.

SHANE

Shane's fetching wood on the mountain,
Shane's off making baskets,
Shane's out to trim vines,
Shane's spreading manure,
and he lugs the bellows to the mill,
and hauls dung to the stable,
and treks to the fountain for water,
and brings the kiddies to mass,
and makes beds and soup...
Shane, in short, is a Shane complete
the kind every woman'd
like at least one of.
But though she look for *Shane*
she almost always ends up with *Pierre*.

Josey, lucky Josey,
the wife of Shane we've well met,
while her husband works
she dangles toes in the creek,
picks lice off the cat,
combs her long hair,
tosses corn to the hens,
gossips with the priest's brother,
finds eggs in the nest,
peeks into the orchard,
licks cream off the milk,
and if she can, tosses back a pint
with her pal, who brings it
hidden under her apron.

And when Shane at night
comes home tired and hungry,
she awaits him in the sheets,
and when she sees him, murmurs:

   —For Gawd's sake, cut the racket,
I'm a total wreck.
—What's wrong, my sweet woman?
—What's wrong? Putting kids to bed,
and this womb gnaws in me
like a dog's gnawing a bone,
and at the end I'm fit only
for the burial ground...
—Oh, my Josey, take a sip
of the herb liqueur I have here,
and sleep, sweet woman,
while the kids are abed.

   And his eyes brim with tears
when Shane sees what's before him;
but don't you fear, in every thousand
there's just one angel amid all the devils;
there's just one tormented
for every thousand who cause pain.

THE MAGIC FLAGSTONE

In dreams of innocence
that free all conscience from remorse,
    with the Virgin at their side,
my angels slumbered in their cradles,
when, furtively, one calm day,
my heart leaping with joy
I went out alone seeking fortune.

I went after a prized treasure,
    no one else even knew of,
I was the only one with savvy,
and it wasn't just of silver or gold,
    that treasure without peer
was all anyone could want.

I was never rich or lucky,
    but I saw I could be so;
I was a hair's breadth from changing
from dry thorn into rose.
    And like a pure virgin
who for the first time feels the sweetness
of the buzz of love, so I was feeling
    that something asleep inside me
was waking, calling me to venture.

And so I forgot
the worries that had consumed me
    since I was born,
I saw earth and heaven tinted with hope,
and around me, eternal spring.

How the sun was shining!
How gently the river murmured!
And the wee bird sang in flight,
    while I walked
    with light step to my goal.

    Whitening like snow,
    there were clothes and bolts of cloth
spreäd on brambles on the mountain,
    oft scattered, oft piled;
just as white clouds dab a serene sky,
lit by sun, they dabbed the landscape
    like no other light.

  By the inlet on its green banks,
    some win and some lose;
while boys played in the toiling waves,
    the guardian angel missed
    one spot nearby,
    and though the boy's parents wept
in his absence as they buried him,
    the old said with compassion:
—He's free now of pain.

  The carts squealed relentlessly,
while the carters slowly sang
    to their rhythm;
    and here a spring flowed,
as there in the quarry, the metallic echo
of the picks of the stonemasons.
Closer, dogs were barking
and the wind stirred in the foliage
from the gulleys to the hills...
What peace! What sun!... What happiness!

—In the end, Luck, you tire,
and though I hunger for my share, you deny me
    my inheritance of pleasure,
granting me worry and quarrels,
    the very ones you want to,
you give me in fistfuls for free.

    This I was saying,
as blissful as could be,
    while I walked
    so happy and sure
of finding the fortune I awaited,
just as I know that to those who seek, God provides.

  Couched in boxwoods and weeds
    the magic I craved
called out like a blackbird in its nest,
over the murmur of rolling waters
    at the distant mill...
    I turned back to the pasture,
followed the path through the broom
and finally arrived!... and on a flagstone
where the crow sits each morning;
    a noble horseman,
jaunty plume in his hatband
and dressed in silk and rhinestones
just like a Moorish swashbuckler,
    called to me cunningly,
    so luminously
that he seemed from heaven, not earth.

  —It's him! I said in trepidation,
    but he of the magic, skilled
for aeons in dealing with women,

not startled at all to see me,
smiled and called me from afár.

   And the sky was rosy as the sun set,
while in the oak woods and gulleys
some quiet breezes blew,
     soft and wholesome,
like promises awaited, now fulfilled.

I don't know what I felt
seeing that he kept calling me,
     half worried and half surly;
     with baleful courage,
I went toward him, full of desire,
like a moth to a candle.

   In his hands, a diamond sceptre,
he tapped on the strange flagstone
that opened, just as seed bursts
     from ripe pomegranate:
     and with soothing voice
     and bearing likewise,
—Let's go! he said generously, onward!

   And I went just as simple leaf falls into calm
current that carries it peacefully
at first in its crystalline waters
to gïve it a loving grave
     on the neighbouring banks,
and then later lifts it, wrenched
     in dark flood,
to the storm-tossed abyss of sea.

I entered thinking I was in heaven!
Why does evil have such power?
   For how it enchants the eye
and hides its ardent desire,
      never tired or full;
there my eyes went, and were snatched up
as never before, and in love.

   For hidden treasure
      with its shine and beauty,
who of woman born,
      what mortal creature
would not have been seduced and fooled?

   And in the light of the half-open door,
without temerity, I was so absorbed,
I stared at the splendid chambers,
one long gallery after another,
and as if I were dead to everything
      apart from what I saw,
I exclaimed in the supreme height of happiness.

   —Here, Creátor, is the universe's treasure
without a doubt;
here is that which is imagined but
      never accomplished.
      Never will anyone else find
treasure bigger, more blessed, or more pure!

   So I blasphemed, without fear or care.
Crazy me, blinded by sin!
And the shine I saw
just as I'd always fantasized
gave me full faith in what I sought.

Thinking that to my good fortune,
heaven on earth had arrived
and the luck I dreamed of had come true,
without a thought for life or death,
forgetting past and present
       and the future altogether,
I only thought of gathering somewhere
all that treasure
unbeknownst to others.

   I stood as high as the powers that be,
forgetting how human nature
is fallible and childish,
and imagining as ever-gushing spring
       these riches upon riches,
and ostentatious and prideful,
I said as I followed the handsome horseman,
—Gïven I found you so easily,
so as to enjoy what's mine later, tell me
where to dive in.

   —Wherever you wish, my lady and queen,
he answered generously
in his gracious voice,
whatever here you love is yours,
but first let's drink, you and I,
from this golden goblet,
for the evils left to us and those we leave,
and the good that smiles on us from the dawn
of an April morning that'll never end.

—Well let's drink! Drink up!
I repeated, befuddled and not from wine,
without first making the sign of the cross
so that the drink would do me good...
and into the fresh and limpid waters
we both went down
>and wet both our mouths...

I will never forget that moment
when immense good luck turned infernal torment,
>as from inside the goblet
>suddenly arose
one serpent's head after another
unloosed, they darted at me,
>and all together
>they rose up at once
>and into my very side
they sank their venomous stingers.

I fell, fell wounded
and almost lifeless,
and still on top of me, they went wild
with their mortal poison
one accursed serpent after another.

>Greát fog spread
in the South, and into the gulley
the pretty horseman vanished;
and a thick cloud swollen with lightning
looming from shadowy Compostela
visible on the far horizon,
just as cold night's dull line is visible
in the dead of afternoon,
confused my simple mind.

    And there above the flagstone
where the crow perches each morning,
I found myself without fortune,
bade farewell to sweet illusion,
alone and wretched like no other creature,
poisoned, sad and badly hurt.

    And I don't know whose rough voice murmured
        in the whistling wind:
        —Like you, foul treasure
        left here by elves
        that greed applauds,
all spells have feet of clay:
for such huge pleasures, huge evil's our return.

*

—We loathed each other so much,
we wished each other so much ill,
that you died so as not to see me,
and since then, I breathe anew.
Now it's my turn
to go and the priest asks
that I forgïve you, for soon
united we'll be again.
The priest's gone mad!
Us together...! Never again, I think;
if you're with God,
I think I'll head to the devil.

This a widow old
and stubborn as a ram,
said of her late husband
already devoured by worms.
And as she spoke,
she too was dying.
But it's said that she and her hubby
found each other again in hell
hand to hand and elbow to elbow
like two long-lost pals.

—How'd you get here?
the widow asked the old guy;
well then, since you've gone to the devil,
I'm going where God is.
And without knowing how
she soared to heaven;

but found the door shut
tight by St. Peter.

—Knock! knock! open up, it's me!
the old widow croaked.
—No way! answered the Apostel,
grabbing the latch.
—But I swore I wouldn't
end up where he is, dear St. Peter...
—No way! the Saint repeated,
retreating inside.
—In the name of your keys,
you sure make a good doorman,
and how you mutter! It's easy to see...
you're pleased with yourself...!

But I gave my oath and God insists
that we fulfill our vows.
For the third time! Will you open up?
—Not at three nor at three hundred;
the wife goes where her husband is:
To hell, go to hell
with him, forever and evermore!
—Bosh, my Saintly dearest Peter,
how can you pretend to judge
when you've always wandered free,
never were you married
not on earth nor in heaven!
You've had every comfort
you could ask for, you devil!
And you won't accord me even one?
For I too want comfort.
If on earth I walked in chains,
there's no way I want chains now,

everything ends with death
just as the priests say.
Once we two split up,
me and my husband, it surely
was forever..., that said,
well I'm just as stubborn as you are.
You don't want me in heaven's glory?
Well I swore I'd not go to hell
where he is; that's it,
and there things stand.
Whatcha going to do with me?
Will I go to limbo with unbaptized babies?
I don't care! I'm areády in it
to the ends of my hair.
—What the haw is up with that woman?
old St. Peter said in anger:
if it weren't for God...
—Phhh, sir, quit haranguing
and let me in...
—No, no and no. Effin'ell!
Get outa here! And pop, he booted her
straight down to hell.
—But I swóre! I areády told you...
screamed the widow, I'm not going in.
Lord, Lord... *sursum corda*;
I'm back, and I'm not budging.

    And she didn't budge, no, didn't budge.
Where? No one really knew,
or knew if it was becaus' God heard her
or because the devil didn't want her.
All we know and know well,
is that she blows on wings of wind
frightening children

in the dark nights of winter,
making lovers jealous,
wrecking weddings,
ruining marriages...
Why didn't St Peter just take her?
For now she walks free and freely
makes our lives a hell.
Keep your fingers crossed, my lasses,
if you hope to have a wedding;
for where she is, not one man
you'll find to save you.

IN CORNES

I

Beautiful field in Cornes,
when you dress yourself in lilies,
you dress my soul
with sombre thinkings.
Of Cornes, such a pretty place,
where roads cross from all over:
although covered with roses,
even roses can be blighted.

Amidst the stones, wallflowers;
amidst the görse, bluebells;
between the mosses, violets;
rivulets between the meadows.
Downstream is the millhouse,
Compostela is upstream....
Upstream or downstream,
all is peaceful in the land.

Bells resound from Conxö,
inviting us to meditation,
oxen drink in your river
and the sun gladdens after rain.
From your earthy houses
smoke rises and roosters crow...
Who in such a fresh refuge
would admit to sadness' stain!

Where there's men, there's sorrow;
but in your fields, my land,
I imagine sorrow is most deep
when you seem most glad.
For those trills of birds,
those echoes, hovering
mists and flowers,
in the sad soul, how they weigh!

   Wandering in wild grasses
I see an orphan girl
who sadly murmurs:
—My Virgin, if I were a rose!
—Why be a rose, dear child?
I asked her warmly,
and she answers smiling,
—Because roses don't go hungry.

   Uphill, up the hill,
we retrace our steps.
We're fleeing this peace,
this enemy of sadness!
What dark contrast there is
between nature's tranquil
rest, and the harsh worries
that slay the simple spirit!

II

   Oh, Cross of Ramírez, you rise stárk
from Agros on the esplanade, between field roses:
the late sun rests its last ray on you
like a golden dream rests on a sad soul.

Sometimes in summer, I sit at your foot
and listen silently, as afternoon ends;
under mute stones that hold your secrets,
I imagine the smooth echo of a harp,
incomprehensible music that speaks of other worlds!

In the same way as at dawn from the Colossus
    of Memnon,
divine sounds are heard, that charm all souls!

III

I hate you, fresh field,
with your green walls,
with your high laurels
and your pale paths
seeded with violets,
shaded by arbours.
I hate you, headlands smoothly
lit by setting sun,
where on serene nights
I've seen the moon blaze,
and where in better days
I wandered among the peaks.
And you too, little
river, more beautiful than any,
how dreary you too
are among my memories...
Because I loved you all so much,
is why now I hate you so strongly!

SAN LOURENZO CONVENT

I

Watching in our fields how
    once again they're tying back roses
    I said: —Where on earth, dear God,
    will I go to hide now!
    And thought of San Lourenzo
    amid silent oakwoods.

Back then those old oak trees,
    their roots emerging,
    their rounded canopies bald,
    and already clothed with mosses,
    spoke to careworn and lonely
    souls, of all that's sad.

The cypress that looms ahead
    behind the convent wall,
    and the slim belltower
    grass-draped and mossy,
    from the pasture with the cross,
    were mute sentinels.

And the Christ who in the stone arch
    bows his weary head,
    lonely, as if still in Golgotha
    wrestling the agonies,
fills oppressed hearts
with resignation.

And if I were to penetrate the cloister,
deserted and in ruins,
never would the world see
a clearer image of oblivion,
or would a greáter silence
on earth surround you.

In the crannies of the hidden spring
digitalis grew freely
between wild violas,
amid boxwood trees;
how pleased death would've been
in that deserted place!

That's why, on watching in the fields
as they tie the roses back again,
    I said: —Where on earth, dear God,
    will I go to hide now?
    And toward the woods of San Lourenzo
    I walked in silence.

II

Where'd my blessed refuge gone?
    I heard strange noise.
    Stonemasons came and went
    through those secluded woods.
    It was as if a pious hand
    cared for the destitute!

In a glance I sized it up inside...
    all glowed white,
    every stone was a mirror,
    and the old convent, a palace
    shawled with pretty flowers.
    How disheartening!

Black clouds fast shadowed
    my astonished eyes:
and wearier than ever,
I fled... ! for my beloved refuge
seemed to me a monk's clean soul
sunken in worldly grime.

March 1880[33]

---

[33] The only dated poem in the collection, it gently but ominously ends the homeland poems. *Rosalía makes of San Lourenzo a symbol of conflictive historical change in which the incipient devastation of capitalism devours all.* (Angueira 444) Angueira points out as well that Rosalía's contemporary, Emilia Pardo Bazán, Galician novelist who wrote in Spanish not Galician, wrote glowingly of the restoration and liked the modernized convent. In March 1880, Rosalía saw the first signs of a future in which cultures would be devastated in the name of economics, to protect capital.

V

WIDOWS OF THE LIVING, WIDOWS OF THE DEAD

ON TO HAVANA![34]

I

They sold his oxen,
they sold his cows,
the cauldron for soup
and the blanket off his bed.
They sold his cart
and the fields he had;
left him with only
the shirt on his back.
—Maria, I'm young,
I'm not going to beg;
I'll go into the world
to try to make good.
Galicia is poor,
so I'm going to Havana...
Farewell, farewell, treasure
of my heart!

II

When no one's looking,
their faces cloud over, sombre,
men like shifting shadows wander
over plains and through fields.
One, on a headland

---

[34] This was the most common destination of late nineteenth century Galician emigrants. Probably, says Angueira, this is the first Galician poem to speak of transoceanic emigration (prior to this, emigration was to Castile).

sits brooding and wistful;
another waits still beneath an oak,
eyes raised to the infinite.
   One, leaning at the fountain,
seems to listen to the murmur
of falling water that mutely exhales
the saddest of sighs.
They're about to abandon their country...!
Forced sacrifice, supreme.
Poverty is dark around them,
oh! and in front of them lies the abyss...!

III

   The sea savagely punishes suffering,
and the irritated waves
of the briny Cantabrian at Coruña
breák against banks of fog.
   Gulls shriek
far out in the distance.... ! so far!,
on placid and solitary shores
where people can relax and love.
   The compact queue of human beings
shines in the sun as it advances and turns;
nearer and more slowly, the path curves
around the ancient city walls at Parrote.
   The heart clenches in worry;
laughter is heard, swearing audible,
and blasphemies mixed with sighs.
Where are those men going?
   In a month, in the immense cemetery
of Havana, or in its woods,

go and see what became of them.
They sleep forever forgotten!
Poor mothers who raised them,
and poor girls who lovingly await them!

IV

—Onward, my buddies!
The whole earth belongs to men.
If you only see what's in front of you
ignorance will devour you.
Onward! God helps those who get moving!
And though we now go far from Galicia,
you'll see when we return
how the oaks kept growing!
Tomorrow's the day, to sea, friends!
Tomorrow, may God protect us!
   Joy in our faces,
in our hearts, fierce striving,
and the harmonious bells of hope,
distant, sound a death knell!

V

   This one went, that one's going,
and all, all of them go.
Galicia, you're without men
to work your soil.
You have orphans instead,
and empty fields;

and mothers who are childless
and children without dads.
And you have hearts that suffer
life-long absences,
widows of the living, widows of the dead
whom no one will console.

NEVER MIND THE DEAD!

I

We'll profane the shade of the woods!
   And before these mute witnesses—
  river, spring, and heavens—
  I swear I'll sever my old ties!
The hours from the past that leaped
  over God knows what abysses.
  They won't return... never mind!
  we can't be martyrs to memory.

II

There's a nest of wild roses
   near the hidden spring,
  and a clover meadow
  carpets the shady surrounds.
For awhile now, breezes stir,
   in the leaves, goldfinches sing,
  the daisies smile upon me,
  and I hear the river's murmur.

III

Without love, this life is dark
   and the sun has lost its shine.
   Let my last sip of all
   be of celestial wine.
It's said that the destitute sleep in the
   ample bed of deep forgetting;
   let's both of us imbibe together
   n these woods among the thorns.

IV

How harmoniously the harsh drone
   of pines resounds in the heights!
   I imagine pines watch us
   serenely from such peaks.
And I seem to glimpse in the mist,
   in the vagaries of the infinite,
   the sad and blurred profile
   of my lost reveries,
and the shades clumsily dráw near me
   through these hills and crannies,
   shades of my beloved dead
   and of my living pain.
But I don't care! From the ancient pasture
   we'll profane these sanctuaries...
   Sit at my side and tell me,
   tell me... what so many've heard.

V

You stand fierce and slender and your eyes
   in mine are steady as stars
   sleeping; they say that love's
   divine touch rests in the eyes.
I look at you serenely,
   my gaze is of cold pebbles
   as I count the turbulent beats
   of your heart.
The atmosphere thickens round us.
   Every day it's the same!
   As birds each have their song
   you, heart, have your rhythm.
But tears inundate my face,
   and deep into my soul
   slow disgust penetrates
   its double-edged blade.
Hey! Stand back from me; I can't
   profane this place of refuge,
   my heart though crazy
   can't murder its own self.
Rest easy, all my angered shades,
   for I am dead to those who are alive.
   Sacred you've remained, oh woods!
   And you, my spirit, are unsullied![35]

---

[35] The woman whose husband has long emigrated almost gives in to the love of another in the woods.

OUR HOME AND NATIVE LAND!

I

Under the placid shade of our good
    country chestnuts;
under those leafy oakwoods
    that make living sweet;
near the fig tree, at my father's house,
    so old no one can count its years,
what happy tales, what loving
    words are spoken there!
Laughter heard in the peaceful evenings
    of loving April!
And there too, such sad farewells
we've so often heard!

II

—To have a house, is alreády to have half a life.
A few tiles for a roof,
four logs to burn in our hearth,
    and endless work!
Courage, courage! And the hope, wretched,
    that while you still have
a few sad walls here, as bare
    and sad as you inherited them,
no one can dispossess you.
    No one? Oh yes, poverty can.

III

Oven without bread, hearth without wood,
    no cricket sings there,
and if it weren't for the aches that gnaw him,
the wretch'd be alone in his suffering.
Without food or coat he shivers,
    because the subtle winds
whistle dank between the stones
    and make all the doors sigh.
What else can be done, Lord, if destitution
    is all around him?
Leave the land that bore him and the house
    in which he hopes to die?
No, no, for winter's done and magnificent
    spring will come.
Already the trees bud in his garden.
    Already April's at the door!
And even though at sad times, there's torrential rain,
    at others, the sun laughs;
already the soil can be sown; the hunger
    of the poor will flee!
Oh! those born in you, beautiful Galicia,
    want to die in you.

IV

Oh, my vines of Albariño grapes,
    gïve me shade!
Oh you, white flowering elder,
    you cure all illness!
Oh, you, all told, my garden so beloved
    and my fields of greens!
I will not leave you, and will banish
    dark worry far from me!
Summer comes to fill all with its fruits,
    all are now rich,
the birds have grain out in the fields,
    shelter in the foliage.
Nights are peaceful and serene,
    the moonlight always clear,
between the rooftiles its rays enter
    and fall on my bed,
and I sleep lit by its lamp
    that gïves light to poor folk:
beautiful lamp, eternally beautiful,
    consolation of mortals.

V

These many mountain paths
    drop into deepest valleys...
There above, the *whoosh whoosh* of wild pines;
    below, sweet peace.
On the peak, clear light, purest air,
    wild solitude,

mysterious sounds that awaken
    thoughts of fierce freedom.
Penetrating perfumes provoke crazy
    strange desires;
belów, in loving calm, the caress of
    breezes stirs
amid the leaves, carrying tales of town
    in their wings,
echoes of some fresh and sonorous voice
    virginal in timbre.
The clamour of the village churchbell's
    prolonged ring,
the rough thunder of the mill dam,
    and the rhythmic thump
as the washerwoman beats white linen
    against a stone.

VI

Yes, yes! God made this enchanting land
    to be lived in and enjoyed;
a paradise in miniature, copy
    of what Adam lost.
This placid sun that gïves us light;
    these breezes from the sea;
this clement air; these tiny fields
    found only here;
the cherished language that is ours,
    such sweet solace,
that it only speaks in utter affection.
    This land touches every heart;

of that there's no doubt..., God made it
>to be loved and to love.
Oh, Galicia, who sleeps the dreams of angels,
>and on waking weeps
tears that, though they console the aches,
>cannot cure its ills!

VII

How your children love you; how it consumes them
>to leave your soil behind;
they sigh inconsolably if they must go
>away to live in other lands.
Though their bodies be in distant regions
>their spirit's always here,
for they live and breathe the memories
>of their homeland.
And they live the hope, the ardent hope
>of being in Galicia again...
And, how can they not adore you so,
>blessed and beloved mother,
how can they not hope not to die far from your breast
>that offers the honey of all honey,
and is glory and joy and paradise
>in this earthly world!

VIII

How beautiful God made you, beloved homeland,
    unlucky beauty!
What tender and melancholy serenity
    I feel when I contemplate you!
Oh why, oh why between flowers must thorns
    be twisted
into the crown that graces your brow
    with evergreen?
Oh Galicia! Galicia! the sonorous harp
    will soon breák free
of the dry branch where it hangs forgotten
    and has slept for centuries.
The bards, your children, will lift their voice
    to the rhythm of its chords
and fill the world with lofty harmonies
    simply to laud you.

*

　　　I wove my cloth alone,
alone my turnip field I seeded,
alone I fetch wood on the mountain,
alone I watch it glowing in the hearth.
Not at fountain nor at pasture,
when I was dying from my load
did he come to help me lift it
nor will he help me set it down.
Sorrow! The wind whistles,
the cicada trills to its beat...;
the cauldron simmers... but, oh my soup,
we two will dine alone.
Shush, turtledove, your cooing
makes me want to die:
shush, cicada, for when you trill,
I feel bleak yearnings.
My beloved man is lost
no one knows where he is...
Swallow who crossed
the waves of the sea with him:
swallow, fly, fly,
come and tell me where he is.

*

    Springs do run dry,
    the oaks let go their leaves;
yet your soul is in full spring:
    all it sees is dawn.

    In vain you hear of the world,
    in vain you hear of life...
What others drink from damned waters
    will not quench your thirst.

    But when your evening comes,
    and your autumn arrives,
come tarry at my tomb,
and lay down your remorse.

HIS PAIN'S NO PAIN OF MINE

Some hurt in wishing to console,
others stick their finger in the wound;
but worst of all is the hypocrite
who keeps intoning: —It'll get better soon!

Those of peaceful conscience
leave us, so happy and serene,
in pain that, even if it won't kill us,
makes life a hell.

But as so often happens,
the one who hurts will be hurt in turn,
claim his pain's as eternal as the Creátor
and fill heaven with his lament.

*

—Just as meat's sold in the market,
    that rotter's sold you out!
—But what does it matter that he sold me out,
    I can't forget him!
—He near killed you, merciless, and left you,
    that turncoat left you.
—I'll die a sad and forgotten woman,
    but forget him... no!
—Like one walks on grass, he walked on you...
    He despised you, and you won't detest him?
—Though he hate me, and walk on me, and curse me,
    I must forgïve him.
—You're so unwavering, you crazy gal,
    you and your loyalty!
But, even if you pardon him, God, who's just,
    won't let him go free.

   (An incredulous bloke, nearby,
grins a devilish grin)
—Trust in God and don't go so fast.
    God! Who knows if there's one?
(An old biddy passing by) —Whoever screws up
will pay, I know, sooner or later.
   (Another guy) —We wander in the dark,
blind to where we're headed.
But grab what you can while it's there to grab,
better to nab than keep on waiting.
   (A roisterer) —There's as many men
as there are thoughts and intentions.
But rare indeed is one who in dying
can forgïve the one who slew him.

*

It was a bone dry Easter, then
rained on the Baptist's Day in June;
to Galicia now a famine
is coming very soon.
With melancholy,
they gaze at the sea with dread;
they who to other countries
now must go to earn their bread.

*

I will not tend the roses
I have of him, nor tend his doves;
they can just wither, as I wither,
they can just die, as I am dying.

*

    I bear an ache
inside my heart;
I bear it, and no one
knows why I do.
Lush banks
of the serene Miño,
where tiny birds
find their mirror,
and sheep graze
amid daisies,
only you know
how I feel.
    Close to a cliff
from where a creek springs,
in the shade of a pine
huge and gentle
that proudly howls
when moved by wind,
my secret sleeps
as if in the grave.
But though it sleeps there
it lives awake in me.
    I bear an ache
inside my heart;
so greát, greater
than, good God, I'd prayed for.
What I would gïve, banks
of the serene Miño,
to be one of those fallow hills
harboured at your side.

Without fears or ache,
in summer or in winter,
one century after another,
they live where I wish to,
with grassy fields for manor,
and spacious sky as roof.

*

My thoughts, how crazily you fly!...
Where are you headed?
Where? Where? If I can't tell,
no one else will know.

From the spring to the river,
from the fields down to the sea.
What do you seek, you crazies? If I can't tell,
    no one else will know.

My thoughts... why do you always
    torment me?
Why are you with me daily, if where you head
    no one else will know?

Like a moth, you seek the flame
    that will burn you up...
and of the sad death you'll come to,
    no one else will know.

I'VE LIVED TO SEE IT

You up and left one day,
you, the one I loved;
you fled the land
that held such joy
and such delight.
You said: —Maria,
sweeter than honey,
prettier than flowers,
my dove unsurpassed,
don't cry, don't cry,
may absence enliven
not kill; don't forget
the sweet love
we were lucky to share.
I'm gone! But if right now
luck's betrayal
brings us grief,
never will I forget you,
so greatly I adored you
so greatly I loved you.
Farewell, my life!
I'll always hold you
in my heart, though
I won't see you again.
Await me, for I do avow
by God most holy,
that if I don't die,
here I'll return.
Die, you did not die,
and though I awaited...

how well you knew
the words you spoke!
Love, what's happened!
The years passed,
flowers withered;
black hair
turned white;
and nevermore, never...
oh the power of a wish!
...did you wish to return:
I've lived to see it.

NOT DEATH'S WAKE

    —You're báck, Rosa of Anido?
Who knew I'd see you so soon!
And all the witches with you, Rosa,
there in the town they tarry,
and you look hálf-dead
and wild-eyed, and your voice cracks.
    —It's just I ache, and from far lands,
bit by bit, I've come back dying;
but... you'll see me flush again,
for now I see you, I feel alive.
    —Crazy Rosa, what's with you!
Do you still recall those days?
    —I still remember! How could I forget,
when they're all I think of.
We drank together at that fountain,
together we rested on that gate,
we gathered hay together in the meadow,
and we went together to take the air
in August when the moon
rose pale over the hills.
These memories consumed me,
away from you and far from home...
But you, tell me, didn't you remember
and don't you remember it all?
    —You ask me, girl, when
I've a memory like a sieve!
And moreover, Rosa, I'll tell you all
so that you banish such thoughts.
I drank with other girls from that fountain,
rested with others on that gate,

and with so many in the August moonlight
did I go to take the air!
Don't you agree, sweets, that a man
weighed down by memories
has to cast them off,
or they'd only cloud his thinking.
I loved you once, Rosa, I did love you;
but as the song goes, love and wind
when they've done their doing,
flee, girl, fast as they had come.
And what are we to do, Rosa,
if that's the way things are?
Farewell! To Havana I embark on Sunday;
and though you cry now, don't fear,
it's heartache, not death's wake,
and, all said and done, time heals.

*

    I want to leave, to leave.
Where to, I do not know.
Fog blinds my eyes.
How can I find my path?
    In such a restlessness
that won't let me live:
I crave and don't know what I crave,
all seems just the same to me.
    I want to leave, to leave.
say some on the brink of death;
oh, they want to flee death,
and death goes with them!

*

    My purest perfume
I'd gïve you were I a rose,
my most serene murmur
if a wave of sea.
The most loving kíss
were I a ray of dawn,
if God... But I aleády know you
want nothing of me, not even glory.

*

—Doctor, her head aches...
Surgeon, her hand is hurting ...
But if it's the spirit pains her,
what medicine will you gïve?
　—For sickness of the soul
there's no cure on earth:
pray to God to take her from you:
maybe in heaven she'll heal.

*

   —Though you serve me Ribeiro wine of Avia,[36]
and all other liqueurs and every dish
on which kings feast and that the world offers,
my dear mother, something's missing.
   Though you hold me in your hands like an icon
and though you clothe me all in finery
and usher me to the Court of Spain,
my dear mother, something's missing.
   And though you gïve me gold, and silver,
diamonds and dark pearls, white pearls and emeralds
all there are in the world, you gïve me nothing,
for, sweet mother, something's missing.
My wings're clipped of beautiful hopes,
and there's no joy where hope's missing.

---

[36] Ribadavia.

*

From here I see the pathway
and I don't know where it goes;
and as much as I don't know,
I want to go and walk it.
Narrow it winds
between meadows and green rows
and at times it's clear, at times hidden,
glinting further on.
But always, always tempting me
with its pretty clarity,
so that I think, I don't know why,
of the towns where it passes,
of the oakwoods that shadow it,
of the springs that will water it.
Pathway, pale way,
I don't know where you go;
but every time I see you,
I want to go and walk you.
You head to Santiago,
you head to O'Portal,
in San Andrés you tarry,
you arrive at San Cidrán,
and in the end, you vanish... who knows
where? How you lure me!
Would that I could vanish on you
and never find myself again...
But you keep going, keep going,
always going somewhere,

and I stay stuck where
my misfortune's rooted.
I don't flee, no, for even if I fled
from one place to another,
from myself no one, no one,
no one will free me.

IN THE CLOISTERS

The doves were kissing,
the sweet swallows flew,
the wind played with the grasses
pocked with daisies,
and the washerwomen sang
as the rivulet ran.
One after another they all went,
and there she remained alone,
with her sad head bowed
near a shady arcade...
Then who knows what shades,
perhaps of vivid memories,
perhaps of departed friars,
passing mystic in procession,
she saw, in those fallow fields
that she both loved and feared.
She trembled from anguish and pain,
and with a bitter smile,
gazing at bare jasmine
that would soon burst into leaf,
she murmured, her eyes
tearful:
—All returns, all turns again,
except the thing for which I yearn,
everything, everything here remains:
I alone try to flee.
I'll no longer see you, flowers,
adorning these cornices;
nor hear your murmurs,
fountain who invites pleasure,

nor contemplate you, stones,
witnesses of my heartache.
Others will come to profane you,
while I die forgotten.
   Footsteps rang out under the domes,
a strong breeze did blow,
there was heard a cáckle
as if it came from hell;
it was the goblin of the cloister
who, remembering other days,
was laughing at bleak worries
and at the orphanhood of the girl.

*

   How her heárt aches,
Oh how much it aches in her!
Neither day nor night
bring halt to her sorrow.
Lord, look what you've wrought;
Lord, cure her!
   And her broken heart,
too, how it hurts her!
And I know well that there's
no cure for heartache.
Lord, let her go to her rest
in the land that raised her;
may dust turn to dust,
and the spirit, to heaven, good God.

*

    The sun come to warm me
gave me shivers,
as if a savage North wind
swept me viciously away.
I heard a bagpipe
happy sounding,
and it gave me
goosebumps;
and I trembled as does grass
on the river bank
when touched by the silts
of the current.
    My aching soul,
my body so simple,
the bagpipe wounds you,
sunlight runs cold.
My soul, my body,
if it's not a curse,
it's that death wants me
for its garden row.

*

    Always you await death,
but death never comes;
poor wretch! Do you think sorrow
kills quickly?
Never, it's like tuberculosis;
after gnawing and gnawing
it leaves a body only when
there's nothing left.
    When the waters of sorrow
pour into the cup without stopping,
      death is the only remedy
      that will cure life.

WHAT'LL I TELL HER?

    —I'm heading home;
what'll I tell your wife Antona?
    —Well, so as not to spark a war,
and so they don't cross the sea to lynch me,
forget you even saw me.
As for the rest... you're free as an ox...
You aleády know the sayings, pal:
freedom first,
and have your cake and eat it too.
    —Better to be bachelor on this shore, as they say,
than married over there with children
and stuck sweating in the corn...
I get it, pal!
    —As far as Antona and her doings go,
and even though I miss her
as over here I neither know nor hear...
Whoever knows and sees nothing... always forgïves.
When I get old,
I'll haul my bones back to the village,
as I have to bring something home to our beloved land;
but while I'm still young, I can't do it,
and speaking of wives,
over there I've got Antona, here Rosa.
    —That one's mother of the year,
my good man Antón of Riaño,
but I'll tell you frankly
that all women are the devil,
and even if that's how it is,
between ours and another's
more or less pleasing,

well...., woman for woman, ours is the best.
　—Ours is the one we love and who loves us,
for when caring is lacking,
you think you've a dove in the nest
and it's really a cobra, daughter of demons.
　—If the cobra's head is split,
it pays with its life.
But take Antona's patience
how will you repay it, in good conscience?
Who'll cure the deep wound of her sorrow?
　—Cut the talk of conscience and sorrow,
they have no place
in talk of women and love.
It's up to her to gët over it if she wants to;
and tell her that when I have it,
I'll gïve her something to get over it with.
And now, farewell, until we meet again!

*

    I have a nestful of crazy thoughts[37]
hidden near the hearth,
and as soon as night comes
and the fire's lit
and I hang the pot and sit to spin
in my favourite spot,
while the soup heats, then I call them:
—Come, my pretties!
    And they run and clamber
all happy to have me to themselves,
to be with their mother, their lady,
their sole affection.
And how we whisper among ourselves
always of him, oh my God!
Of him, who's gone..., and left me
with an aching heart.
    How many sorrows, how many
deep sighs of lament
have tormented me! How many,
right from my heart!
But all in secret,
for we speak of it to no one;
It's unthinkable that I should murmur
of what he's done to me.
    Talk of you to just anybody...me?
Never, my sweetheart;
you are my husband and I your wife, and I must
hush my grief at your straying.

---

[37] This poem is the eerie twin of the preceding poem.

I confide only in my own crazed thoughts,
for they are my friends
and so discreet, so much so
that they say only what I allow.
    Without them, my Joachim, what'd become of me?
Alone here, when once I was with you,
bursting with sorrow, as thorns
burst in the fire!
    Many times, yes, many...,
so as to keep me awake, those rotten thoughts!,
they come into my bed,
and where you slept, they nestle;
but I, as I do now,
so as not to cry me a river
and so as not to get up at dawn
with eyes red as burning embers
when I go to market,
I know to call them despicable.
Stop tormenting me and go hide
in your little burrow!
And I bid them farewell in passing
with a loving kíss...
But though I kíss them, the kíss
is for you alone, dear Joachim.
    Come back, back to me, for though I claim
I can live consoled
by my crazed thoughts, perhaps,
perhaps they're leading me to death, oh my God!
    Joachim, Joachim, born of a woman
and with children from another,
oh! as your father'd have died without your mother,
I'm dying without you, dear Joachim.

ONE DEATH WILL DO

Hush, black dog, don't howl
at the door of the one I cherish;
crows, don't fly across
the roof where he lies ill.
You who glow, you *wandering souls,*
get lost, don't make him fear.
If it's that you wish someone to die,
I know of one robust who gladly
will trade lives with him
and go with you to hell.

TORRES DE OESTE[38]

   The river runnels
on its way,
and I went toward it
near Laíño,
weak with the sorrows
that abide in me.

   With such a burden,
where was I going?
The Virgin might know
what I don't know;
but perhaps it was myself
I was fleeing.

   Amidst hayfields,
deep and shady,
like a serpent
with burnished scales,
it glinted in my eyes
making me greedy.

   I was so alone!
Not a boat or launch,
nor sail nor oars
brightened the view,
and the meadows too
were all alone.

---

[38] A ninth century fortress at the head of the Ría de Arousa, the western Galician bay where the River Ulla meets the Atlantic. Its name means 'The Western Towers' and it marks a potential point of departure, a sill or aperture: to emigration, or—in the other direction—to Galicia.

How lovely were
the roses once
that in those fields
bloomed and dropped petals!
But then they withered,
every one.

And sun, like moon
on a night of mist,
glowed trembling
between basket-willows,
pallid
as wax.

Dark and tossed,
the waves lashed out
and in the black density
of the depths,
long wet seaweed's seen
making its furrows there.

Suddenly one thing and another
make me afraid,
and I saw the struggle
of crosses
that rise along the shore
as if in a cemetery.

My love, where are you?
I asked in tears.
Now you've died,
what in the world will I do,
like you, oh towers!,
alone without harbour?

Loneliness consumes me,
tears feed me,
shadows accompany me,
sadness devours me.
Who can live with such
greát grief?

And I know not what dark
damned temptation
froze my spirit,
clouded my sight,
and smiled on me like
only the devil could.

From the deep banks
I looked around...
The rising tides
lapped at the towers,
orphans in the liquid
sheet that engulfed them.

—I'm going there! I told them.
—Gïve me sweet death,
waters where sadness
sleeps forever...
I leapt, and the deep
current carried me away.

. . . .
. . . .
. . . .

Oh, Torres de Oeste!
Evil temptations,
leaden waters
of treacherous calm,

stripped headlands
where the crow rests.

    Oh, Torres de Oeste!
So alone and mute,
here you witnessed
my sorrow.
No one sorrowful draws
close to you ever.

    To the abandoned
you pay your homage,
and even air
does not well up
near you, as if it feared
to bid you farewell.

    It's the women
whom your sadness touches,
those whose hearts are heavy,
daunted women,
whose struggling souls
are on the path to hell.

    And if I'm still alive,
it's because a mariner
pulled me from the waves
by my hair,
half moribund,
into the world in which I yearn.

    Don't ever go,
is my advice,
to the Torres de Oeste
with darkness in your heart.

WHY?

    —Hark! the bailyffes
are bearing down on the village;
but how to pay, how? if one can't
    even pay the rents?

They seize everything, for those people
have no conscience or soul.
    We'll be out the door,
    children of my womb!

    May foul death fell you
    before you set foot here!
    The hearts of the poor, on
hearing you, beat so sadly!

    —Mary, if there weren't
a Maker who rewards and punishes,
    I'd slay those men
like a fox does a hen.

    —Silence! Don't blaspheme,
    for this is a vale of tears...!
But why do some have to suffer so much,
and others lives their days in plenty?

*

She's dying of yearning
in town, pining for the village;
the houses with their walls spooked her,
as did the towers and churches.

The cobbled streets seemed to her
without green or freshness,
a cemetery where the dead
wandered outside their sad graves.

And food tasted to her
of flour without salt and of bitter radish,
and she had so few meals,
instead of giving energy, they were killing her.

At times, I don't know if in reality
or dream, scents of rural fields
reached her from
distant riverbanks and pinewoods.

She went then to sit upon a rise,
contemplating the wide horizons,
and, breaking into sighs that drowned her,
exclaimed in hoarse sobs: —I'm going!

And off she rushed without a second thought! Went
with the mortal sorrow that consumed her!
Poor Rosa went off
but... to another life!

*

　　—Oh, Rosa, take heart,
life brings great aches
to those who live with gusto,
and forgotten will be she who was beloved.
What happened to you, happens to us all
in one way or another.
　　Don't you remember that lass?
All in her was charm and beauty,
all innocence so pure;
and with deep tenderness
and with a love that could soften stone,
I always called her
my peerless dove, and fount of caring.
It was as if the dove nursed at her breast,
which was so white, it glowed!
And perfume, colour, savour, and I fully
relished all Angela's flavour,
though I didn't even dare to breathe her scent.
Everything about her was blessed to me!
　　That was long ago, a happy time
and my heart still cherishes its memory,
for after that
and with both of us living apart,
she gone to Ferrol and I to Cambados,
we'd try to meet at the Campelo Fair,
and though I struggled to find, in her face
and in her whole being,
that charm which once enchanted me,
I couldn't feel it any more.

    Yet she was the same, tall and pretty,
so fresh and flushed,
and sweet as honey from the hive;
but to all her spells
I was immune,
and I sought in vain from the past
a changing phantasm that fled
free of love and free of chains.
    I meditated a moment,
and with certain remorse and feeling,
I finally realized, my dear Rosa,
that whatever charms I'd fallen for,
they were nothing to me
and that my love had lent her
other charms than those she really had.
    For wisdom is not enough,
nor generosity, beauty, nor innocence,
purity, nor virtue:
to be well loved and to love well,
being suffices on its own.
    While love abides,
even if you're ugly, there's no woman like you,
none more amiable or better looking;
even if you seem horrible and lost, you'd be blessed
among those who are without trying to be;
even if you're a foolish bore, it's that
you have a hidden essence blessed with grace
inside a mysterious reliquary
where only the blind and visionary lover
finds the essence or elixir of life.
    But when love flies away, my dearest,
when its blindfold falls,
we have to let love go,

for there's no virtue or power that can hold it,
and the ones who once saw us through a cloud
or transparent bubble,
once the bubble bursts and the cloud passes,
Rosa, it's best they do not look on us.

BURDEN OF SORROW

So many wildflowers in the valleys,
such festivities and lace
spring up from moss and greenery;
what colours, what foliage in the trees
while breezes gently flit
like the breath of ángels!
In the meadow reigns a placid calm,
the light falls on the creeks in flashes,
and headlands and ravine deftly
carve the landscape,
lightly cloaked in mists
of mysterious afternoon.
All that's heard is the chirp of birdies,
the murmuring of waters,
and on the mountain top, the sad song
of a woman walking,
while the gentle creek accompanies her
in its rhythmic monotone murmur.
What sadness so sweet!
What solitude so peaceful!
But for a soul utterly orphaned,
what solitude so deserted and so bitter!

    She gazes without looking
    into the distant mists,
    vaporous and light
    as the sun paints them red,
    and with hands clasped, and eyes
    raked by tears,

she murmurs sobbing: —I want to leave,
for I'm dying here disconsolate...
    Rather than here amid roses
oh! I want to go to die where he has gone.
    And in the ship's hold
      alone, abandoned,
in love and toward death, to America
to die of grief, she heads to sea.

SO ALONE

    Both far from home
we wander and suffer, for sure!
But you in your loneliness remember home
and I, remember home and you both.
    Both of us wander the world
and our strength gradually fades,
But, oh! in home you'll find your rest,
and I will find mine only in death.[39]

---

[39] The widow of the living lives herself a kind of death. In the last three poems of this 'book outside the book' that ends the book, we see that she (the woman, the I) must either forget, go follow and try to find her emigrant lover, or prepare for death.

Translator's Acknowledgements

Thanks to Jonathan Dunne and Small Stations Press; my translation was made possible due to Jonathan's enthusiasm, encouragement, understanding, and feedback.

Thanks to the organizers of the *Canada & Beyond 4th Biannual Conference 2016* at the Universidade de Vigo for the opportunity to speak about Rosalía's contemporaneity in the age of precarity and migration in which we live today. Both of those are particularly hard on women, in our time as in Rosalía's.

Big thanks to Karis Shearer for tolerating my disappearance into the nineteenth century over the 2.5 years it took to translate these leaves. Many thanks to Belén Martín and to Oana Avasilichioaei: their quick response and detailed feedback enabled me to vastly improve my introduction.

Thanks to POEM (UK, ed. Fiona Sampson) and to The Capilano Review (Canada, ed. Andrea Actis) for publishing poems from the manuscript. Great gratitude to Anxo Angueira and Helena Miguélez-Carballeira for their generous sharing of their books, the new Xerais edition of *Follas Novas,* and *Galiza, Um Povo Sentimental?,* respectively. Both books nourished my work in introducing *New Leaves*; Anxo Angueira's superb notes to Rosalía's poems were key in my final revision of the English versions. I feel lucky indeed to have such companions, for no cultural work is the product of one mind alone.

Finally, I would have been unable to translate *Follas Novas* or *Cantares Gallegos* without two amazing tools available to me on the web. One is the *Dicionario de dicionarios: Corpus lexicográfico da lingua galega,* created and maintained by the Seminario de Lingüística Informática at the Universidade de Vigo (Computational Linguistics Research Group, special thanks to Antón Santamarina and Xavier Gómez Guinovart) and supported by the Instituto da Lingua Galega. The other is the *Dicionario RAG*, a Galician dictionary available for free in app stores (iOS and Android) thanks to the Real Academia Galega (RAG) and the Fundación Barrié.

Index of Titles/First Lines

A child trembles in the damp portal   194
A Rolling Stone   142
A true love is greát and blessed   131
Alert!   133
Always you await death   273
And so! When your most   146
At night's apèx, there   58
At the Manor of A...   101
At the Tomb of English General Sir John Moore   155
Be brave! For though you're pliable as wax   151
Beside the flowers, the girl   139
Burden of Sorrow   288
But see that my heart   68
Dig quickly, dig down   97
Doctor, her head aches   265
Don't sing, don't cry, don't laugh, don't talk   132
Every night I pondered tearful   83
Faded Moon   110
Farewell!   75
Field crickets, mole crickets, pale wee cicadas   76
For each beat, another   66
For life and for death   154
Frigíd months of winter   170
From here I see the pathway   267
God's cast a veil over   105
Good Loves   86
His Pain's No Pain of Mine   252
How her heárt aches   271
How placidly they glow   111
How the clouds in open space   77
Hurry, Álvaro of Anido   186
Hush!   199
I bear an ache   256
I Crave You, You Crave Another   148
I go in search of honey and freshness   70
I have a nestful of crazy thoughts   276
I know well there's naught   52
I once had a nail   60
I want to leave, to leave   263
I will not tend the roses   255
I wove my cloth alone   250
I've a sickness that's incurable   190

293

I've Lived to See It   259
Immense elms, myrtles   136
In Cornes   229
In the Cathredal   79
In the Cloisters   269
In the skies, blue so clear   102
In the sway of May, long May   109
It was a bone dry Easter, then   254
It was in the month of May   171
It's true any person can   192
Just as meat's sold in the market   253
Just like clouds   53
Keep Going   117
Lead me to that clear fountain   100
Luck Betrays   99
Mandolin Song   182
May this cup from which you drink   85
May you end up, by God   189
Mean Loves   87
My purest perfume   264
My sweet abode, my hearth   200
My thoughts, how crazily you fly!   258
Never Mind the Dead!   241
New Leaves!! It makes me laugh   55
No Charge   89
Not Death's Wake   261
Not in the Dark!   134
Now hair of black   188
Of Any Curse, There's No Worse (Than Heartbreak)   123
Of women who write of doves and flowers   51
Oh, Rosa, take heart   285
Old Friends   107
On to Havana!   237
One Death Will Do   278
Open wide, new roses   88
Our Home and Native Land!   244
Padrón...! Padrón...!   114
Pallid virgins with candid faces   184
Peace, peace so craved   59
Pleasure, for scabies, relieves the itch   191
Poor woman so deaf...!   205
Prideful   203
Race on, serene and crystal waves   82
Rich or poor, back then   78
Ruins (*translation of Ventura Ruiz de Aguilera*)   178
Sad Recollections   166
San Lourenzo Convent   232
Scared, I see the abyss   153

Sea! with your fathomless waters   96
Shane   215
She's Alone!   119
She's dying of yearning   284
Silence!   71
So Alone   290
Some say: my land!   57
Some see black   164
Springs do run dry   251
Squeal of carts from Ponte   181
Stranger in Her Own Land   112
Sweet Sleep   152
That hum of song and laughter   64
The Hand of Justice   103
The Magic Flagstone   217
The Peal of Dawn   94
The sun come to warm me   272
They howled at me as I walked on   91
Though you serve me Ribeiro wine of Avia   266
Tick-tock, tick-tock! In night's silence   106
Time to Get Drinking   130
To Everything Its Time   138
Today or tomorrow, who knows when?   62
Torres de Oeste   279
Unnestled   147
Vanity   185
We loathed each other so much   225
What'll I Tell Her?   274
What's this buzz around me??   56
What's Up?   176
When I think you've gone   98
When it was winter   67
When one's very joyful, very joyful   61
Who Wouldn't Sigh   90
Why, God of pity   118
Why, sweet soul of mine   93
Why?   283
With its deaföning and constant mormur   69
With no rancour or disdain   63
With what grace you sway   160
Without Earth   163
Woe   143
Yesterday You, Tomorrow Me   84
You claim that marriage   187
You write some verses and... what verses!   193
You, charming and white as snow   177
You'll say of these lines, and it's true   54

Index of Titles/First Lines in Galician

A bandolinata   182
A disgracia   143
¡A probiña, qu'esta xorda!   205
A un batido, outro batido   66
A ventura é traidor   99
A xusticia pó-l-a man   103
Abrid'as frescas rosas   88
¡Adiante!   133
¡Adios!   75
Agora cabelos negros   188
Ala, pó-la alta nòite   58
Alguns din, ¡miña terra!   57
Amigos vellos   107
Amores cativos   87
Ando buscando meles e frescura   70
Anque me des viño d'o Riveiro d'Avia   266
Apresa Alvaro d'Anido   186
Aquel romor de cántigas e risas   64
As Torres d'Oeste   279
Basta un-ha morte   278
Ben sei que non hay nada   52
Bós amores   86
Brancas virẍes de cándidos rostros   184
C'a pena ô lombo   288
Caba liẍeiro, caba   97
Cabe d'as froles a nena   139
Cada cousa no seu tempo   138
Cada noite eu chorando pensaba   83
¡Cal as nubes n'o espaço sin limites!   77
Cal grasiosa brandeas   160
¡Calade!   199
Cand'era tempo d'inverno   67
Cand'un é moi dichoso, moi dichoso   61
Cando penso que te fuches   98
Chirrar d'os carros d'a Ponte   181
Co seu ẍordo e costante mormorio   69
¡Cómo lle doy á yalma!   271
¡Como venden á carne n'o mercado!   253
¡Corré serenas ondas cristaiñas!   82
D'aquelas que cantan as pombas y as frores   51
De soidás morriase   284
De valde   89

Decides qu'o matrimonio   187
Deixa que n'esa copa e'n donde bebes   85
Dend'aquí vexo un camiño   267
Dios puxo un velo enriva   105
Diredes d'estos versos, y é verdade   54
Dor alleo n'é meu dor   252
Dulce sono   152
¡E ben! cando comprido   146
E verdade que un pode   192
En Cornes   229
Era n'o mes de Mayo   171
Espantada, o abismo vexo   153
Estranxeira n'a sua patria   112
Eu levo un-ha pena   256
Eu por vos, e vos por outro   148
Fas uns versos... ¡ay que versos!   193
¡Follas novas! risa dame   55
Foy á Pascoa enxoita   254
Grilos e ralos, rans albariñas   76
Ladraban contra min que camiñaba   91
Lévame a aquela fonte cristaiña   100
Lua descolorida   110
Mais vé qu'o meu corazon   68
¡Mar! c'as tuas auguas sin fondo   96
Mayo longo... Mayo longo   109
Medico, doill'a cabeza   265
Meses d'o inverno frios   170
Meus pensamentos cal voás tolos   258
Miña casiña, meu lar   200
N'a catredal   79
N'a tomba d'o xeneral ingles Sir Jhon Moore   155
N'é de morte   261
N'hay peor meiga que un-ha gran pena   123
¡Nin as escuras!   134
N'o ceo, azul crarísimo   102
N'o craustro   269
Non cantes, non chores, non rias, non fales   132
Non coidarey xa os rosales   255
O encanto d'a pedra chan   217
O meu olido mais puro   264
Ó pazo d'A...   101
Ô sol fun quentarme   272
O toque d'alba   94
¡Olvidemo-l-os mortos!   241
Os manantiales sécanse   251
Oxe ou mañan, ¿quen pode decir cando?   62
¡Padron!... ¡Padron!   114
Para a vida, para a morte   154

Para uns negro 164
Pasade 117
Paz, paz deseada 59
Pelouro que roda 142
Pois consolate, Rosa 285
¿Porque, Dios piadoso? 118
¿Porqué, miña almiña? 93
¿Porqué? 283
¡Prá á Habana! 237
Premita Dios que te veẍas 189
¿Que lle digo? 274
¿Qué pasa ò redor de min? 56
Que pracidamente brilan 111
¿Qué ten? 176
¿Quen non ẍime? 90
¡Querom'ire, querom'ire! 263
Rico ou probe algun dia 78
Ruinas 178
San Lourenzo 232
Sarna con gusto, non pica 191
Sempre pó-la mort'esperas 273
¡Silencio! 71
Sin niño 147
Sin terra 163
Soberba 203
¡Soya! 119
Tal com'as nubes 53
Tan soyo 290
Tanto e tanto nos odiamos 225
¡Tas-tis! ¡tas-tis! n'a silenciosa noite 106
Tecin soya á miña tea 250
Tembra un neno no húmedo pórtico 194
Teño un mal que non ten cura 190
Teño un niño de tolos pensamentos 276
¡Terra a nosa! 244
Ti onte mañan eu 84
Tí, a feiticeira e branca com'as neves 177
Tristes recordos 166
Un verdadeiro amor é grande e santo 131
Un-ha vez tiven un cravo 60
¡Valor! qu'anqu'eres como branda cera 151
Vamos bebendo 130
Vanidade 185
Vivir para ver 259
Ẍa nin rencor nin desprezo 63
Ẍan 215
Ẍigantescos olmos, mirtos 136

GALICIAN

CLASSICS

1. Lois Pereiro,
  Collected Poems

2. Álvaro Cunqueiro,
  Folks From Here and There

3. Celso Emilio Ferreiro,
  Long Night of Stone

4. Rosalía de Castro,
  Galician Songs

5. Xosé María Díaz Castro,
  Halos

6. Rosalía de Castro,
  New Leaves

Erín Moure
is one of Canada's most eminent poets and translators. She has won the Governor General's Award for her poetry, and the A.M. Klein Prize for Poetry twice. Her translations, two of which have been shortlisted for the Griffin Poetry Prize, include five books by the widely recognized Galician poet Chus Pato (the latest, *Flesh of Leviathan*). She has also translated work by Andrés Ajens, Nicole Brossard, Wilson Bueno, Fernando Pessoa, François Turcot – and the first major book of poetry by Rosalía de Castro, *Galician Songs*.

www.ingramcontent.com/pod-product-compliance
Lightning Source LLC
Chambersburg PA
CBHW030231170426
43201CB00006B/175